THE UNSEEN INDIRA GANDHI

THE UNSEEN

INDIRA GANDHI

Through her physician's eyes

DR K.P. MATHUR

Konark Publishers Pvt Ltd
New Delhi · Seattle

Konark Publishers Pvt. Ltd
206, First Floor,
Peacock Lane, Shahpur Jat,
New Delhi-110 049.
Phone: +91-11-41055065, 65254972
e-mail: india@konarkpublishers.com
Website: www.konarkpublishers.com

Konark Publishers International
8615, 13th Ave SW,
Seattle, WA 98106
Phone: (415) 409-9988
e-mail: us@konarkpublishers.com

Second Impression 2016
First Published 2016

Cataloging in Publication Data--DK
Courtesy: D.K. Agencies (P) Ltd. <docinfo@dkagencies.com>

Mathur, K. P., 1923 or 1924- **author.**
The unseen Indira Gandhi : through her physician's eyes / Dr K.P. Mathur.
pages cm

ISBN 9789322008727

1. Gandhi, Indira, 1917-1984–Friends and associates. 2. Prime ministers–India–Biography. 3. Mathur, K. P., 1923 or 1924- 4. Physicians–India--Anecdotes. I. Title.

DS481.G23M38 2016DDC 954.045092 23

Inside photographs courtesy: Author

Editor: Sivadas Sankar

Typeset by Saanvi Graphics, Noida

Printed and bound at Thomson Press (India) Ltd.

CONTENTS

FOREWORD

For all the years of my grandmother, Indira Gandhi's Prime Ministership (and the brief interlude from 1977 to 1980), Dr K.P. Mathur was a part of our household. My brother and I would come out of her room every morning having wished her before leaving for school to find him waiting outside the door in the company of her wily valet, Nathu Ram. Often we would exchange glances and the good doctor would ask Nathu in a conspiratorial whisper, "*Bhai, aaj mijaaz kaise hain*?" Nathu would impart the required weather report with a wry smile on his face, "*Sab theek hai*" or the occasional, "*Aaj to Bibiji bade gusse mein hain*", and word would go around the entire household to prepare itself for the tides of the day.

Over the years, Dr Mathur, or "Doc", as all of us fondly referred to him, became more a member of our extended family than just a part of my grandmother's entourage. His keen sense of humour and his ability to grasp the finer details of human emotion endeared him to all of us. He had a particularly perceptive way of interpreting my grandmother's disposition from unlikely clues like a raised eyebrow or the slightest gesture of her hand. To his credit, he forged a relationship with her that enabled him to speak freely to her without the diffidence that some of his colleagues never managed to shed. I think my grandmother welcomed this frankness and reciprocated it with an obvious sense of respect towards him.

His place in her household gave him the unique perspective of being an insider while also being able to see things from an objective distance. As a result, his memories of that period remain filled with a rare quality of humanness. In his narrative, aspects of my grandmother's personality that have been less written about—her sense of fun for instance—feature alongside her fearlessness and fallibility.

During our childhood, Dr Mathur was a storehouse of fascinating tales for my brother and me. He would recount to us, his experiences on official tours with astute observations regarding those surrounding our grandmother and regale us with anecdotes about various sycophants and hangers-on. On foreign trips, we often ended up in his car in the convoy accompanying our grandmother, or in a room adjoining the one allotted to him. His companionship on these occasions was always welcome. He is now 92, and still blessed with a sharp and lucid memory. I am glad that he has decided to put down his memories as a tribute to a brave woman whom we both admired, to the times that he witnessed and the long years of his loyal and dedicated service.

March 04, 2016

(Priyanka Gandhi Vadra)

PREFACE

Mrs Indira Gandhi, a towering personality in a petite frame, remained an enigma to many a people. I was privileged to have a long association with Indiraji and as her physician, was able to view at close quarters, many different aspects of her personality.

A number of friends had been asking me to write a book on the subject. However, I felt that given her status as a leading world politician and statesman, many books had already been written. It was pointed out that although a lot had been written about Indiraji, it was largely about her as a politician, an administrator and the policies she administered. The incidents and anecdotes that I narrated informally, always captivated the audience of close friends. After many years, they were successful in persuading me to collect all these incidents and personal conversations with her and compile in the form of a book.

Hence, this book—*The Unseen Indira Gandhi.*

After the unfortunate and fateful morning in 1984, when we both walked out of her house—me towards my car and she into the volley of bullets—a lot of time had elapsed making the task of compilation rather difficult and laborious.

Indiraji had a habit of writing instructions and messages on bits of paper. Without giving any thought, I had collected quite a few of them, which came in handy to jog my memory about the time gone by. I have shared a few in the book to provide a glimpse of yet another side of Indira Gandhi. Amongst the several things that I learnt from her, the one that stayed with me forever, was the importance she gave to being thrifty and economical.

This even came through in her writing of personal notes or letters. What her speech writer took several sentences to express, she would do in a few words! Her wisdom, deep compassion for people in suffering was another. She would often come forward with her advice that nobody in this world will ever be so rich to not need any help; nor ever be so poor to not be able to give help.

I have endeavoured to present to the readers, scenes of what went on behind the scenes. From her lifestyle, relationship with family, friends and other world leaders, to her disposition during stressful times, the book makes an effort to reveal the true personality and character of the woman who charmed the world.

During my association with her, I was fortunate to meet many accomplished personalities from around the world. The book has references to some of these who helped shape many events during Indiraji's lifetime and thereafter.

I do hope this book provides readers a glimpse into 'Indira's world'; a world unknown to many.

लोक - सभा
LOK SABHA

Report on the Human Zoo.

1. Sleepy as a bear in winter.

2. Eating like a pig.

3. Constipated as a cat (only because of the alliteration!)

Dr Nathan

3.5.72

NOTE 1 When the recommendation that a physician be appointed for her was made, PM had joked that she didn't need a doctor but a veterinarian as she lived in a human zoo and that she was sleepy as a bear in winter, eating like a pig and constipated as a cat (only because of the alliteration).

ENTER THE DOCTOR

I am often asked how I became Indira Gandhi's physician and managed to stay in that position for nearly two decades. My answer to the second question is that Indiraji was, generally, a forgiving person and perhaps, I also did not make any unpardonable mistakes to warrant dismissal. I am certainly not perfect but my shortcomings were generally overlooked.

Indiraji was, on the whole, physically fit and relatively young (49) when she became the Prime Minister first in 1966. She was not keen on having a personal physician and therefore, no doctor was appointed in that position for the first few months of her tenure. But as chance would have it, on one occasion, when PM was returning from a tour, the aircraft she was in ran into some turbulence and lost balance. The impact was felt inside the cabin as well, as a result of which some people were thrown off their seats. A few were quite seriously injured; they were bleeding and in great pain. Everyone then felt that had a doctor been on the spot, he could have at least administered first aid to those injured. PM also felt the need for a doctor who could deal with such an emergency. Immediately on return from the tour, she asked her private secretary, N.K. Seshan, to have a word with Col. R.D. Ayyar, Medical

Superintendent of Safdarjung Hospital, and ask him if he could nominate a doctor. The general elections were scheduled for 1967 and PM had a busy tour programme and hence, it was necessary to sort out the matter as quickly as possible.

Seshan got in touch with Col. Ayyar. By chance, when Seshan's telephone rang, Dr Prem Kumar Mishra was sitting with him in the cabin. Col. Ayyar took Dr Mishra into confidence and told him what the call was about.

Ayyar's immediate reaction was, "What about Mathur?" Mishra agreed with the suggestion but advised him to first define the job requirement and then think of a person suitable for the job. By that time, I had been a doctor to a number of senior politicians, bureaucrats and other VIPs and they all thought well of me and had a good word for me.

Nevertheless, Col. Ayyar listed a few qualities that anyone being considered for the post had to possess. One was, of course, to be a good doctor, above everything else. Secondly, he had to be extremely discreet and not go about bragging or throw his weight around by virtue of being the "PM's doctor".

The third condition was that he had to be well-mannered. At this Mishra laughed and asked, "Sir, who will not be well mannered in the presence of a Prime Minister?" Col. Ayyar responded, "Dr Mishra, I do not mean well-mannered in the general sense, rather in the Lucknowi style: *aayiye; tashreef rakhiye; hukum kijeeye; khidmat ka mauka deejiye*" ("please come, be seated; let us know what you need and allow us to be of service"). He remarked that he had seen me deal with such people and that I was very good at those mannerisms. Col. Ayyar was a Malayali like Seshan but was brought up and educated in Chennai. He could hardly speak any Hindi or Hindustani.

On all the three grounds, I got an okay from both Col. Ayyar and Dr Mishra and my name was passed on to Seshan. When Seshan informed PM about Col. Ayyar's recommendation and mentioned my name, PM said that she vaguely remembered one Dr Mathur who used to come to see her husband Feroze Gandhi, when he was admitted to Willingdon hospital (now Ram Manohar Lohia hospital) and she thought it might be the same person.

Seshan got in touch with me and asked me to go and see PM. I met Indiraji that same evening; I had met her a couple of times earlier but was meeting her as Prime Minister for the first time and hence, I was a little nervous.

Some relatives of hers were also waiting in the room to meet her. On arrival, she greeted them first and then looked at me and asked "*aap*?" I mumbled, "Col. Ayyar has sent me". I was unable to speak any further out of nervousness. Seeing me thus, she called out for Yashpal Kapoor, her PA, who came running and told her that I was the doctor Col. Ayyar had sent. "Oh, you are the doctor! Why not say so?" she asked, obviously amused at my discomfiture. Bowing to the other guests, she took me to another side room. She asked me if I knew what had happened in the aircraft that morning and added that she did not require any doctor for herself but an emergency like that could arise any time and a doctor is required to give at least some first aid to those injured.

She then enquired if I was willing to take over the responsibility. I agreed at once; still, she advised that I should think well before accepting and also told me that in the coming months, her schedule was going to be pretty hectic, going on tours for most of the days. She was also concerned about my family's reaction, how my family would take to my new responsibility. "Do consult your wife and other members of the family before giving a final reply," she told me. She asked me to see her after two days as she was leaving on another tour. When I met her the next time, I had no hesitation in accepting the assignment. In fact, I submitted to her that I considered it an honour to be of service. From that moment on and till the last moment of her life, I remained her doctor and with her.

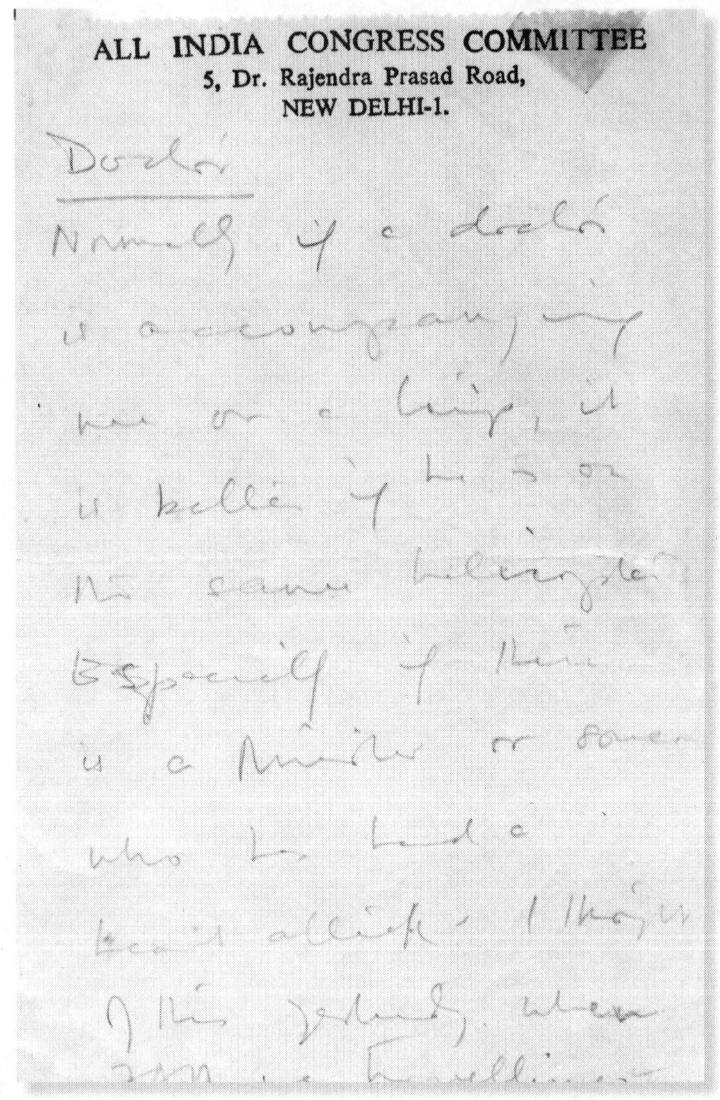

ALL INDIA CONGRESS COMMITTEE
5, Dr. Rajendra Prasad Road,
NEW DELHI-1.

Doctor

NOTE 2 Her stance changed a bit later and she said that if there is a doctor among us, they should even travel with us. She realized the need for one at hand when Fakhruddin Ali Ahmed, who had not been keeping too well, travelled with her.

SPARTAN LIFESTYLE

When I first entered PM's house, I found no influence of Lucknowi culture in her style of living which reflected in the way household affairs were managed.

PM was quite a pleasant, caring and helpful person. She tried to see the good in everything and in every person. She was seldom critical of anyone but if she truly disapproved of some person, she would use very mild language, like "he is a peculiar person" or "a funny man." She never used strong language against anyone.

She often conversed in Hindi or Hindustani as it was spoken by cultured families of UP or North India. A patient listener, she always addressed her interlocutor directly as *bhai* (brother). Those who spoke to her were usually satisfied with the quality of the interaction, even if they did not get a long audience.

Everyone was treated with due consideration. The servants were treated well and each one was addressed by his or her name. There was an elaborate call-bell system connecting the rooms and the pantry where the servants generally stayed. Nobody was shouted for, and yet instructions were given, though never in the form of orders or commands. Her two old Anand Bhavan retainers, Kali Prasad, the valet, and Ramkumari, the maid, did not fear to differ from PM's views and used to make suggestions in a tone and temper as if they were better than her. PM often conversed in the local *Allahabadi* dialect, *avadhi* with these two and then used to feel very satisfied thinking her fluency in French and English had not detracted her from her facility with her own tongue. Ramkumari always referred to PM not as madam or *Behenji* but as *Bhayyaji*, perhaps in keeping with the tradition that the first born in the house, even a girl, would be treated as a boy. In fact, PM used to refer to herself as a boy in her childhood; she could be seen dressed as a boy in many family photographs.

PM's style of living was simple, not aristocratic. There was no sign of opulence. Thrift was her guiding principle. She continued to stay in a small house which was allotted to her when she was a minister in Lal Bahadur Shastriji's Cabinet. She had lived the best part of her life earlier in a grand style first at Anand Bhavan and then at Teen Murti House. Her friends tried to persuade her to shift into Teen Murti House but she resisted all such attempts and continued to stay where she was; a couple of rooms were added when Rajiv and Sanjay got married so they could have some privacy.

Her own living quarters consisted of a fair-sized bedroom with an attached bathroom, wall to wall carpets and an air conditioner. The furniture was maintained in first class condition. The adjoining veranda was enclosed and served as her sitting-room-cum-residential office and library. Books were stacked all over the place. PM used to sit now and then on a *diwan* to browse through the books. There was an office table, a revolving chair and two stools where her PAs sat down when she summoned them for dictation.

I had the occasion to see PM herself changing the bedcovers on the *diwan*. It was the day after the Bangladesh War had started and she had worked late into the night. When I went to see her in the morning, I saw her engaged in the exercise of dusting. Perhaps, it helped her release the tension of the earlier night. Another thing which intrigued me during my early days was a yellow rectangular mattress spread on the floor. I couldn't understand its purpose. I asked her PA about it. She told me that PM used it for her morning exercise and yoga. One day, she noticed me looking at this mattress attentively and before I could ask anything, she told me its history. She said that during the freedom struggle, they had to travel in third class coaches of trains and the mattress was custom-made to fit the rail compartment berths.

However, she added that during those days she could never use it as the wife of a prominent Congress leader would always take possession of it while they were travelling.

Her drawing room was elegantly furnished with furniture of good quality and expensive carpets, apart from it being fully air conditioned. It was decorated with wall paintings and other items borrowed from the National Museum, subject to return and replacement. It was cleaned and dusted every morning and every thing was put in its proper place. It remained locked and was opened only when the President or the Vice-President called on PM's birthday or when some top foreign dignitary was visiting. It used to be locked immediately thereafter. For daily use, there was another room which was also decently furnished. Sundry visitors, ministers, governors, political leaders and top officials were received here.

Her dining room was furnished by the Public Works Department with their furniture and upholstery. These included a large dining table which could accommodate more people when the need arose, by attaching a separate section.

On all such occasions, PM was very particular that everything was done tastefully: furniture, furnishings, cutlery, flower arrangements, etc. She would supervise the menu to ensure that all the guests enjoyed the meal. Even at her private dinners in the house, she wanted everything to be perfect. She would review the seating arrangements too so that everyone enjoyed the food and the company. Even for the official dinners at Rashtrapati Bhavan, where the staff was trained and experienced in such arrangements, she would go through the menu and seating arrangements. On one such occasion, J. Jayalalithaa, who was an MP then, was invited but assigned a seat way down the main table, well away from the chief guest.

PM was quick to realize that she was a rising star on the political firmament of the country and bound to go up fast with her personality and political acumen. She saved the situation by getting her to leave the designated place and sit closer to the centre of the table and nearer the chief guest. How right her hunch was about Jayalalithaa! Today, she rules the state of Tamil Nadu in immaculate style, and is often counted as Prime Ministerial material.

Indiraji was not highly educated in the conventional sense. She had not passed any examination at a university to entitle her to attach a BA or MA degree after her name. But she had been to two of the best universities of the world, Vishwabharati and Oxford where she studied for a couple of years but did not pass any examination. She had, however, a string of honorary doctorates from some of the best universities in the world.

She was a voracious reader and her knowledge was vast and varied. She could hold her own in the company of the best academics anywhere in the country or abroad. I had the opportunity of seeing her in such company.

The schedule of meeting intellectuals on tours was followed just as much as when PM was travelling abroad. Wherever she went, a programme to meet the intellectuals was arranged. In many places, a good number of such persons would assemble to meet her; sometimes the number could be quite large and I could see her moving in their company with grace and ease that comes out of inner confidence and satisfaction. Most times, these people used to gather in small groups with PM moving amongst them. She would make it a point to say a word or two to each one of them because she was aware of their works.

In metropolitan and bigger towns, thinkers were found easily, like authors, journalists, lawyers, professors and the like. But where does one get such intellectuals in a small town with whom PM could interact? Once in a small town in UP, this programme was held and was attended by about 10 people, 3 or 4 being ladies. PM started the meeting by asking them to tell her their views about the current problems of the country and what were their reactions and probable solutions for them. In response, there was a chorus "madam, give us your '*sandesh* (message)'." And the same was repeated a number of times. PM kept on saying that she keeps giving her sandesh so often and everywhere and now, they should tell her their thoughts. This went on for some time and the meeting was not making any headway. In the end, PM said, "you tell me something and you will get both rasgulla and sandesh (sweets)!" The meeting still did not progress and ultimately PM made her usual speech and said, "here is your sandesh, OK?" Everybody had a good laugh at PM's sense of humour.

PM loved her children, grandchildren and her daughters-in-law. Sanjay would be busy with his car project and later, in local politics which in course of time extended into the national sphere. Rajiv spent a good bit of his time as a flier and devoted his spare time with his family and friends. After Rajiv's marriage with Sonia, PM was very keen that Sonia should get into the social and cultural life of the country.

Towards that end, she had given instructions that everybody should speak in Hindi/Hindustani at all times. In the morning, when the cook asked her about the menu for the day, she would refer her to Sonia saying, "Please ask *bahurani* what she wants".

She was quite free playing Holi with members of the family, friends and other personnel of the staff in the house. Whenever possible, she used to attend Dussehra and Diwali festivals as organized by local Ram Lila Committees. Sometimes, small children from local schools would come to sing Christmas carols in the house. They were very welcome and duly entertained. Likewise, Muslim friends were greeted with Eid Mubarak during the festivities. Some of them would thereafter, send *kebabs, biryani* and *saevay*. If I happened to go to PM's house during that time, I would also get a taste of these delicacies.

PM was very particular about observing birthdays of her family members or her immediate family friends and associates. As far as possible, she made it a point to be at home for her birthday because she did not like to disappoint all those who would come to greet her. Every time, a hundred or two hundred people would come with bouquets to greet her on her birthday. One person who used to make these arrangements quietly behind the scene was her *mali* (gardener) who would always come quite early in the mornings and ensure that the decorations were made with flowers and buntings with leaves; flower pots were arranged all over the place to give the house a new look. PM would mix with all the people who assembled, speaking to as many as she could and accepted their bouquets. She used some of these to decorate the house while others she personally handed over to me to take home, because she knew that my wife was interested in flower arrangements, especially the Japanese Ikebana. She also once presented a complete book on the subject to my wife. The rest of the bouquets, I was supposed to carry to the hospital for distribution among patients. She could not tolerate flowers being thrown away or trampled upon. As for the birthdays of members of the family and friends, she remembered them by heart. Those of others were recorded in a separate register and the PA on duty at that time would remind her when the day arrived. She would then call up in person. Sometimes, she would start with some humorous remarks; for example, her lady secretary, Mrs Usha Bhagat, was fond of music and dance. When she called Usha on her birthday, she would start the conversation by asking if she woke up that morning singing or dancing. She was on very friendly terms with Usha Bhagat because once I saw her dancing while greeting PM on her birthday. On another occasion, she phoned her friend Mohammad Yunus and asked, "Yunus, have you counted the number of grey hairs in your beard?"

In my case, a couple of times she sent a formal greeting card signed by her and members of her family. On another occasion, we were not in Delhi but in Colombo and to my great surprise, one of her PAs brought a paper on which she had written a poem for my birthday, "We all know a Doc /who works round the clock /with his mixtures and pills /he cures all ills."

Temple Trees
Sri Lanka 18. 8. 76

We all know a Doc
Who works around the clock.
From backache to colds, he
cures all ills,
With ointment, massage and
multicoloured pills.

On his auspicious birthday
From family & friends he is faraway.
So we join to give him best wishes
For health, happiness and just plain
riches!
Whatever he may covet,
Let him have it & love it!

ROUTINE CHALKED OUT

As PM's personal physician, I was supposed to look after her health and that of all other members in her family and household. I had to be with her on all the tours within the country and abroad. (I remember that on tours within the country, PM was aware that people lined up on both sides of road to have a close look at her. They assembled with the earnest hope that they would be able to see her. Just to oblige those who came to see her, she made it a point to sit on the front seat next to the driver. During the day, it was all right because the sunlight was enough for people to see her. But even after dusk or during the night, there were people still on the road waiting to have a glimpse of her. PM had devised her own method of showing her face to those who had assembled. The security staff would carry a battery torch during all her tours. Sitting on the front seat, she would place the torch on her lap so that her face would light up for those outside to see her. Occasionally, she would even wave her hands to greet them.

During important public functions, meetings, and Independence and Republic Day celebrations and other such occasions I had to remain as close to her as possible and follow her around. I remember a lady who was curious to know how I became PM's physician and what my duties were. Upon hearing my answers, she seemed to feel some sympathy for me and remarked, "But it must be quite boring!" I told her that it was not at all boring and that it had its rewards. Still not satisfied, the lady persisted and asked, "How do you feel following PM all the time and everywhere?" I replied, "Like Mary's little lamb!"

As PM's physician, I used to see her every morning. These visits lasted barely a few minutes and were more like courtesy calls.

One day, it occurred to me that I should familiarize myself with the history of PM's past illnesses. When I broached the subject, she agreed but since it would have taken some time narrating the history and answer my queries, she herself suggested we meet on Saturday for this. This was perhaps because on Saturday she could take it easy and had some time of her own as she did not have to go to office.

On the scheduled day, she narrated the whole history of her past illnesses; she remembered every detail and easily answered all my queries. Just as we were about to finish, she thought of a minor ailment she had suffered towards the end of her first pregnancy. Trying to be a little funny, I enquired, "When Rajiv was on the way?" Without missing a beat, she replied, "No, Rajiv had almost arrived and was knocking on the door; I delivered the next day."

To make sure that PM enjoyed good health, I wished to see her at least once a week and also do a brief clinical examination. Even the briefest of such an examination takes at least half an hour or 45 minutes which PM was not able to spare except on Saturdays. After some persuasion, she agreed to let me see her every Saturday for a longer check-up.

Later, it occurred to me that she should also be examined by some doctors independently, and undergo the necessary investigations, akin to a thorough medical check-up.

When I told this to PM, she did not agree immediately. Her first reaction was that she was fit and fine and I had been examining her every week so there was no need for another check-up.

I told her that independent doctors would be examining her so we could have an objective view. Finally, she relented. I requested the professors of medicine, surgery, gynaecology and pathology, all from AIIMS, to conduct the check-up. Since the examinations, including laboratory tests, were to be done early in the morning, PM was fasting as per the requirement. The doctors had also not eaten yet. The seniors were accompanied by their assistants along with technicians and nurses. The examinations took almost an hour. After blood had been drawn for laboratory tests, PM left after thanking every one of them and sat for breakfast in her room. I ordered some tea and biscuits for the doctors and others. When I went inside to tell her that everything seemed all right, she enquired if something was offered to the doctors. When I told her about the tea and the biscuits, she exclaimed, "This is no breakfast." The next time, a proper continental breakfast was served to the doctors. On another occasion, she suggested a South Indian breakfast. Once, the typical desi breakfast of *puri kachori* and *aaloo ki tarkari*, along with *jalebi* from Chandi Chowk was served. A couple of times she joined in the breakfast. She was a gracious host and the doctors and their assistants were absolutely delighted having breakfast with her; they felt honoured to have PM serve them.

PM was particularly solicitous about the health of some of her friends, namely Pupul Jayakar, Mohammad Yunus, Pitambar Pant and, especially,

Padmaja Naidu whom she respectfully addressed as "Bibi". Pupul was quite fit and healthy, though her husband was not so fit and would often need some medical help or the other.

Yunus was a hefty Pathan, physically and emotionally robust. Pant was quite ill but kept his problems strictly to himself and did not even inform PM for a long time. One late evening, PM called me to say that Pant was very ill and asked if I could have a look at him straightaway. In fact, she herself took me to see Pant, who lived near her house. The next day, he had to be admitted in AIIMS where PM visited him several times.

Padmaja was a vivacious elderly lady, interesting and fun-loving. PM had great regard for her in view of their long family relationship and felt responsible for her well-being. She was often down with minor cold, cough and chest problems and PM expected that I would go and see her. Once, she got ill with a rather bad attack of flu and had to remain in bed for about a week or so. I went to see her a number of times. During one of these visits, she asked me about my family and when I told her that my family consists of my wife and four daughters she was surprised.

"No son?" she asked and I nodded in assent. A few days later, when she got well, she came to see PM when I also happened to be there; she thanked both of us profusely for our help. Later, talking about her sickness in the course of the conversation, she referred to my four daughters and no son as if it were something strange and a hitherto unknown fact. PM had a good laugh. Looking at the curiosity and anxiety on Padmaja's face, but pointing towards me, she said, "*Bibi*, can't you see, that's why he looks so hen-pecked!" The two ladies kept laughing at my discomfiture. Padmaja Naidu was in splits and clapping, having made a great discovery that there can be a man with four daughters and no son, and PM at her own wisecracks.

PABA

Inositol (Lecithin)

Pyridoxene (B^6)

Pantothenic Acid

Use one Tablespoon pure inositol in a glass of fortified milk for prevention of baldness.

NOTE 3 A prescription for PM

SPECIAL REGARD FOR ARMED FORCES AND SCIENTISTS

PM had special consideration for our defence personnel and scientists. She always found time to attend their meetings, Annual Day celebrations or other programmes.

She always attended the Army, Air Force and Navy Day functions or special displays they would put up. I went with her for two years when she went to witness the naval exercises.

On both occasions, she spent two days with the officers and men of the Navy. They would arrange special parades or sometimes cultural programmes or evening parties, dinner in the Officers' Mess and the like. Once on board the *INS Vikrant*, even some air display was also arranged. While on-board the *INS Vikrant*, she was interested in watching the landing and taking-off of the aircraft and marvelled at the precision with which each one of them at a time would come on the deck quietly, rising out of the ships' bellies.

One very cold December morning when I went to see her, she came up with a strange proposition that within a few days, she would like to make a short trip to Ladakh. On hearing this, I was taken aback a little as a visit to Ladakh which is at a height of 3000 ft in such freezing weather was not advisable for her health. I tried to dissuade her and suggested that she should make the visit in June or July when the weather would be a little more favourable. Her response was, "Look doctor, everyone wants to visit Ladakh in summer but someone should also visit it during this time of the year to find out how our jawans fare in such a snowy climate and at that height." It was not just words but a genuine concern for the jawans that she exhibited there.

It appeared at first that the visit had been put off but a couple of days later, I learnt that on my advice it had been fixed within the next few days; it was to be a day's trip. I was worried not so much about the cold, but rather the "high altitude sickness" which could strike anyone not acclimatized to those heights. Here was a major cause of concern for me. I went to have a word with Gen. Hoon, an army doctor who had made a special study of high altitude sickness, especially with reference to our troops stationed at those heights. Gen. Hoon first laughed at me for arranging PM's visit to Ladakh in such cold weather and only for one day at that. He told me that the troops were moved up in a gradual and systematic way while travelling to Ladakh, taking at least a couple of days to reach, which allowed them to get acclimatized to the atmosphere. I told him that the visit had been fixed; he advised that I should administer a tablet of Lasix to everyone before landing at Ladakh.

On our way to Ladakh, I administered the medicine to the members of the party, including PM. Lasix reduces the volume of the blood which helps in curbing high-altitude sickness but it also makes one prone to immediate and frequent urination. Being aware of this, the Air Force had made some arrangement for PM in the helicopter itself. I had warned everyone about the drug and its side-effects but its efficacy was evident almost immediately. Everyone was feeling uncomfortable and some had their faces contorted. As soon as the helicopter landed and the door was opened, they all just jumped out and ran in all directions to find some place to ease themselves. Protocol and manners were forgotten; it is usually PM who alights first. She appeared quite amused with what was going on. Nevertheless, the day's programme started as per schedule: the usual introductions, guard of honour and all that. She had lunch with the officers in the mess. Thereafter, she addressed the jawans and there were separate meetings with senior officers and others after which she returned in the evening, all safe and well. In the aircraft, she enquired from me about the peculiar behaviour of the people in the morning on our arrival at Ladakh. I explained to her in detail that this was the effect of the medicine. She had a good laugh but chose to believe that I had played a prank on everyone, notwithstanding my protestations.

She made another trip to Ladakh but this time I was a little more careful about administering Lasix to avoid any *tamasha* (drama) as on the previous occasion. She spent a full day and night there looking into the various activities of our soldiers. At the same time, she did not forget the larger civilian population. To meet them, she went around the town and drove to the local market, reciprocating their cheers and greetings. She also went to visit some old monasteries located in the interior parts of Ladakh. She had a special fascination for temples and monasteries.

Once during her visit to BARC (Bhabha Atomic Research Center), she was scheduled to go around the plant and also address the officers and men working therein and was accompanied by Dr Raja Ramanna, the then Head of BARC. While they were organizing the programme of PM's address to the staff of BARC, Dr Ramanna and I were sitting in a corner and talking.

In the course of the conversation, Dr Ramanna asked me, "Doctor, tell me where does she get all the energy to do so much in a day and go around all the time"? I replied, "Sheer will power".

PM had seen us talking to each other but before the address she casually asked me as to what I was discussing with Dr Ramanna. I told her that we were wondering about how she was able to do so much. She responded by asking as to what my reply was.

In the course of her address she mentioned all this and what Dr Ramanna had asked me. She said that her answer to that is, "I have atomic energy; and not only me, but all of us have this atomic energy. But some use it gainfully and others let it go waste. My advice to you people would be to use your atomic energy in the service of the country. The nation expects a lot from you."

Many requests were made for PM to inaugurate or address many medical conferences. PM readily agreed to most of them. Since such requests were made through me, and therefore I was in the know of things, except once when she had some hesitation that the delegates would be experts in their field and I should let them choose a person amongst themselves who will deliver the keynote address after which discussions could follow. Such a thing happened about two times. But, PM nevertheless, showed her participation by visiting them or seeing their exhibits and at least once she invited all the delegtes for tea at her residence. All the delegates, numbering about 100 attended and they were delighted by PM's presence and her hospitality.

Once on a trip to an army post in Himachal Pradesh, the helipad happened to be very close to the Officers' Mess. PM was to have breakfast there. After we landed, all of us were taken to the Army mess where she addressed the officers but it was really an informal talk, and she tried to give them a chance to feel at ease and say whatever they wanted to say. The commanding officer, wanting to impress PM with the range of his knowledge, monopolized the conversation and kept on talking about all kinds of things, jumping from one topic to another. Ultimately, he started to narrate about how the city had been invaded by monkeys. He said they were not scared to enter even the area under the army's control.

Continuing in this way, he added that usually a clever burly monkey would come forward and take the lead and the others would follow him. He used the phrase *pradhan* (chief) monkey for the monkey leading others and said things like, "when the *pradhan* monkey jumps, they jump like him" and so on. We were controlling ourselves with great difficulty but finally, everyone burst into laughter. The man realized his mistake and apologized profusely. PM laughed it away by saying, "I don't mind being your *pradhan* monkey, if you all are monkeys".

Ask Doctor if
I should take
a Dristan now
I feel a cold
coming on.

Dr Nathan

R.B.
Darjeeling
21.11.75

NOTE 4 PM asking me if she should take a Dristan for the cold she feels is coming on

FOOD PREFERENCES

PM's penchant for economy and thrift was seen everywhere. For example, on tours on her aircraft whenever breakfast was served it consisted of *vada, chutney*, sandwiches, one or two seasonal fruits and coffee, all this stuff brought from the South Indian Coffee House in Connaught Place. Once, the Minister for Civil Aviation happened to be on board with PM. When this breakfast was served to him, he was a little surprised but somewhat unhappy. He called PM's PA and questioned him, "Can't we even serve a decent breakfast to our PM?"

The PA informed him that the menu was according to PM's own choice and that it had been the same since Panditji's days. Without asking anybody, the Minister ordered Centaur Hotel to provide breakfast on every tour PM undertook. On the next tour, breakfast packets sent by Centaur Hotel were served to all, including PM. On seeing the packet, she called the PA and asked him about this "novelty". The PA informed her that this was done at the behest of the Minister for Civil Aviation himself. PM asked, "What was wrong with the earlier arrangement?" However, she had the Centaur breakfast all the same without further questioning, not wanting to disappoint the Minister, as was her wont.

Though PM had no fads about her food, whenever she went on tours to different places in the country, she preferred to savour the local cuisine or food cooked in local style. For example, when in the Southern states, she preferred South Indian food or coffee; in Gujarat, dishes like *dhokla, khakra*, etc.; in Rajasthan, local dishes like *dal bati, churma*, etc. Once, in Murshidabad in West Bengal, for lunch the normal *dal roti* and *chawal* was served for her but she could smell fish being cooked in mustard oil, ready to be served. She immediately asked for it and had a liberal helping of "*mach-bhat*" and liked it very much. Similarly, once on tour in the interior parts of Himachal Pradesh, she was invited for dinner where the food was cooked in Tibetan style with yak butter put in the soup. She took a full meal not sparing anything. I was a little apprehensive that this unaccustomed food may cause some stomach upset and wanted to give her some medicines as a preventive step but she refused, saying "the food was very good and I quite liked it, and so nothing will happen to me, don't worry."

Once on a tour of Andhra Pradesh, during election time PM had to stay in Hyderabad for two or three days at a stretch. We were staying at the Raj Bhawan where our rooms were on the first floor and PM's suite was also on the same floor. PM would be served all her meals in her dining room but for the rest of us, there was a common dining room on the ground floor. One morning, when I went to see PM, as I did every day, I found her sitting in her dining room waiting for her breakfast, which was brought in soon after. Since it was breakfast time, I wanted to leave so that I could also take my breakfast with others, but PM, being kind and considerate, suggested that I could also get my breakfast in her room and join her.

I told her that I would like to go down (to the common dining room) and eat there with others. Light-heartedly and somewhat surprised at my preference, she enquired, "Is there something more or extra or additional being served there that is not served here?" I knew what she meant, and replied, "No, not that, but they (other members of our party) will be waiting for me." On reaching the breakfast table, I found there was the usual bread, butter, fruit, tea and some hot *idly, vada* and *upma*, so I preferred to take some of the latter and washed it down with a cup of hot coffee. After finishing my breakfast, I went to see PM again, just in case she had something to tell me. She had nothing special to tell me, but asked, "So you finished your breakfast; what did you have?" I told her about the South Indian fare which I had taken. Hearing this and surprised and as if protesting, she exclaimed, "Look they cook such nice cuisine—*idly, upma, vada* and other things for breakfast, but for me, they bring only toast and butter, they don't get the other things for me, why?" It was almost like a school girl complaining about "discrimination". After waiting for a few moments, I tried to explain, "perhaps *idly, vada*, etc. is their everyday meal but they think this is not good enough for VVIPs from Delhi, there should be something special for them, that's why?"

"Is this special?" she asked pointing towards the breakfast table, and "this coffee, there is such nice South Indian coffee, but for me, they bring this tin of Nescafe." A little later in the day, I met the keeper of the Raj Bhawan and remembering PM's remarks, advised him that whenever they made *idly, dosa, vada, upma* and such things for breakfast, they should send them to PM also who liked them. "These we make every day for our other guests, but I will send some for her," he agreed.

The next day in the morning, there was a knock at my door and as I opened the door, who do I find but the Governor of Andhra Pradesh with two tiffin carriers, one in each hand! He said, "Doctor, I have brought some *idly* for you," and handed over one tiffin carrier to me; the other, he said, was for PM. I asked him, "Sir, why did you take the trouble, there is everything in the kitchen." It seems some distorted version of the morning's incident had been relayed to the Governor for him to take things in his own hands in this way.

Two or three days later in Andhra Pradesh again, an election meeting had been organized by the local Congress Party, at a place quite near Hyderabad. Incidentally, there was a defence production factory close to the venue. The public meeting was scheduled to be held early in the morning. The Defence Ministry was very keen that PM pay a short visit and also inaugurate an exhibition they had arranged, either before or after the meeting. PM had agreed to accommodate their request. She had her breakfast early that morning before leaving for the public meeting. She reached the venue, addressed the meeting and went on to see the exhibition at the defence factory. Since it was breakfast time, it was expected by the officers that PM would take her breakfast with them in their mess. But time was running out and she had very little time for the mess. They tried hard to tempt her saying that they had some hot *idly, dosa* and *upma* ready. Perhaps the information about PM's preference for South Indian breakfast had reached them. PM kept saying that she had already had her breakfast. Time was running short and she had moved to the exhibition area while they were still insisting on breakfast. Not one to disappoint her hosts, PM asked them that whatever they had prepared be brought where she was. "I will take it here", she said.

Quickly, somebody brought some plates, spoons, etc. there and two or three plates full of *idly* and other items. Since I was also standing there, they gave me a a plate too and another plate piled with *idlis* to her. She kept saying, "Look, I can't eat so much, somebody should share". Since I was standing nearby, she told me, "Doctor, you should share". She pushed one or two into my plate. "That is enough", I said. "Take some more", she insisted. I was fumbling for a spoon but she advised, "Pick some with your fingers". I picked one or two and put them in my plate. All this happened in full view of the people around.

Everyone was perplexed about who this man could be whom PM herself was offering food to; he seemed to be eating out of her plate! My share price shot up immediately. Later, while we were leaving, a senior officer from the defence factory came up to pick up my medical bag and carry it to the helicopter. Another remained with me throughout the day to help despite my protests about it being unnecessary.

If Dr Mathur – still here, please tell him I have a bit of a tummy upset. Have we any pills here? Shall I take Stelabid? P.M. 9/5/75

NOTE 5 PM wanted to check if I was still there and if she should take a Stelabid for her tummy upset.

THE DAILY DRILL

PM did not take any bed tea. Her food habits were simple. The day started with a simple breakfast consisting of one or two slices of bread, well toasted (slightly burnt) with a little butter, a half boiled egg and some seasonal fruits, an apple or a banana and some milky coffee. This she would normally take about half an hour to finish, after which she would look into any urgent files placed before her by the PA or read the day's newspapers. This lasted another thirty minutes after which she would go out to meet a visitor or two who had a prior appointment or she met members of the citizenry. These public meetings came to be called *darshans* (holding court); about a hundred people would collect on the lawns of the adjoining house to her official residence 1, Akbar Road; there was no restriction on visitors and anyone could see PM at that time. All these people who came to see her had some problem or grievance and required help.

Often the problem presented was about someone being ill, and requiring medical assistance, including admission to AIIMS. People came from far and wide. At AIIMS, the number of beds were limited and people had to wait sometimes and spend a couple of days on the footpath till a bed became available for admission. PM handed over such cases to me and it was my duty to look after their admission and treatment in any way possible. The *darshan* would go on for about an hour till it was time for PM to leave for office or Parliament, when it was in session. PM was very particular about her parliamentary duties.

She used to come for lunch at about 1.30 or 2.00 p.m. Her lunch was also quite simple; usually a vegetarian meal. After resting a little, she would go back to office. For dinner some meat or chicken was also cooked sometimes or ordered from outside. At times, some of her Muslim friends would send some nice preparation cooked in their homes. This occurred more during the Ramzan period. After Sonia came to live in the house after her marriage, she would often cook some Continental dishes which PM greatly relished.

Sometimes, when I happened to be in the house, PM would often call me to the dining table and offer whatever was cooked or something else that was laid out, like sweets, fruits, chocolates or things like that. I would take whatever I liked.

One item cooked in her kitchen which I particularly liked was *kurkuri bhindi* (crisp fried ladyfinger): *bhindi* wrapped in *besan* (gram flour) and a special masala, fried crisp, quite like *bhindi ki pakodi* (balls of ladyfinger). One evening, when I was called to the dining table, I found there was *kurkuri bhindi* on the table, and when PM asked me to help myself, I immediately agreed to take some *kurkuri bhindi*. She asked the cook to "get some *kurkuri bhindi* for Doctor Sa'ab". The cook went inside the kitchen, returned empty handed and gestured that *kurkuri bhindi* was finished. PM's immediate reaction was "doesn't matter" and immediately, picking up her plate of *kurkuri bhindi*, she pushed the entire portion onto my plate with a spoon. I tried to make light of the matter and said that I would have it some other day, but she was insistent. I felt it would be improper to have her entire share so I requested that she take at least a few pieces of the vegetable back. She took back two or three pieces from my plate, smiled and said, "Okay, its fair". I was overwhelmed by her courtesy and the regard that she showed towards me. By this act of generosity, she had made me her *"hum niwal"* (fellow eater).

PM was religious minded and a traditionalist. Part of her religiosity was inherited. Her grandmother, Sarup Rani, was a disciple of Anandmayi Ma. PM would also visit Ma now and then. Ma had given her a rosary made of *rudraksha* beads which was supposed to ward off evils. PM almost always had it on her person. I also once visited her *ashram* near Haridwar.

Later, in her religious thinking and spiritual activities she was guided by Swami Dheerendra Brahmachari, a yoga guru who used to visit her quite often. Popularly called Swamiji, he was well versed in Hindu texts and scriptures and legends. At breakfast time, he would often sit down with PM at the dining table; on other days it was at her office table where she would take her breakfast and look into files.

Swamiji did not eat anything solid but drank a large tumbler of milk and also used to have a good helping of fruits and burped loudly much to PM's annoyance. He would relate stories connected with he Mahabharata and other epics, apart from the history of famous temples in the country. Another person who came to influence PM in religious matters was Harsukh Pandit. His knowledge about the country's temples was phenomenal and he had information about many temples in the Himalayan region about which others might not even have heard of. Once he accompanied PM on her tour to the South and on another occasion to Uttarakhand to see famous temples.

Harsukh was a fair, tall, well-built person with penetrating blue eyes and silken grey hair; a very impressive personality whose presence no one could ignore. I am not sure whether PM performed a regular pooja every day but she had framed pictures and small statues of many gods arranged in a separate room with a small mat on the floor, presumably for her to sit on and pray. She would make it a point to visit every famous temple in any part of the country during her tours. I invariably accompanied her during those trips. She prayed at the Badri–Kedar, and many South Indian temples. She had visited Tirupathi several times, as well as Vaishno Devi, always fully observing the prescribed rituals. While visiting the Golden Temple after Operation Bluestar, she ordered two dozen caps from the khadi bhandar for each one of us to have proper headgear and not the formal handkerchief which most would tie over their heads on such visits.

Lately, whenever I am
in the sun, I get an
itch on my hands.
I have put on the
anti-sun lotion.
For Information

NOTE 6 Lately, whenever she was in the sun, she felt her hands itch for which she started putting an anti-sun lotion.

FEROZE GANDHI

It was no secret that PM's relationship with her husband Feroze Gandhi were strained. Feroze Sa'ab was rumoured to have a glad eye and this was always a matter of strain in their relationship. Feroze Gandhi was a very friendly, informal and talkative person. He was also quite handsome, fair and had an overall attractive personality. People of both sexes were easily attracted to him. He was a leftist with a strong sympathy for the common people. The couple were living separately, PM with her father in PM's house and Feroze Sa'ab in the MP quarters some distance away.

However, very few people might have known that despite the differences between the two, PM continued to have very cordial relations with his family. She regularly observed the Parsi New Year, Navroz. She often enquired about their well-being from Usha Bhagat, who had come to know the family well over the years and had developed cordial relations with them. Once, PM even went to Bombay to attend a family wedding and spent a whole day attending all the ceremonies and in-between, also running out two or three times to fulfill her official and party engagements. In the evening, there was a dinner to which all the members of her party were also invited. This was the first time that I savoured some typical Parsi cuisine.

Sometimes in a casual conversation, a reference would come up about Feroze Sa'ab and such incidents were generally related to their holidays in Pahalgam. She would immediately brighten up on hearing someone talk of those days. One of her favourite stories was about the time Feroze Sa'ab fell off a horse.

She had organized a picnic in the morning while holidaying in Pahalgam with Feroze Sa'ab. She had carried some hot coffee, fruits and other edibles, cutlery, a mat to sit on the grass, and one or two towels, etc. They were sitting when Feroze Sa'ab came from the other side on a horse, and dismounted at the spot where they were sitting. He lost his balance and fell down on all fours. His jacket was soiled and there was mud on his body; luckily he did not get hurt. She asked him to take off his jacket so that she could brush it clean.

Whenever she narrated such incidents, she would break out laughing, remembering the fun she had. It appeared as if she was talking of an estranged friend in whose company, she had enjoyed many moments of genuine happiness.

There was a cartoon by the famous cartoonist Shankar of Feroze Sa'ab sleeping at 12 noon on a Sunday, wrapped in a razai, with sun rays streaming through the window. She got the cartoon framed and kept it near her home office table. Once, when she noticed me looking at it, she narrated the story of how Feroze Sa'ab forgot about an appointment he had made with Shankar to meet him at his residence. Instead, Shankar found him asleep; he woke him up and gave Feroze Sa'ab a good scolding. She narrated this story while laughing throughout.

On another occasion, when she saw me looking at this cartoon again, she narrated the whole incident forgetting that she had already told me in detail; it was as if ruminating on this incident again left a pleasant taste in the mouth. This cartoon is probably still there at its original place at the Indira Gandhi museum.

Differences apart, PM had also not forgotten her duties towards her husband. I remember clearly when Feroze Sa'ab was admitted to the Willingdon hospital (Ram Manohar Lohia hospital) with a heart ailment, I went to see him two or three times and every time I was there, I found Indiraji attending to him.

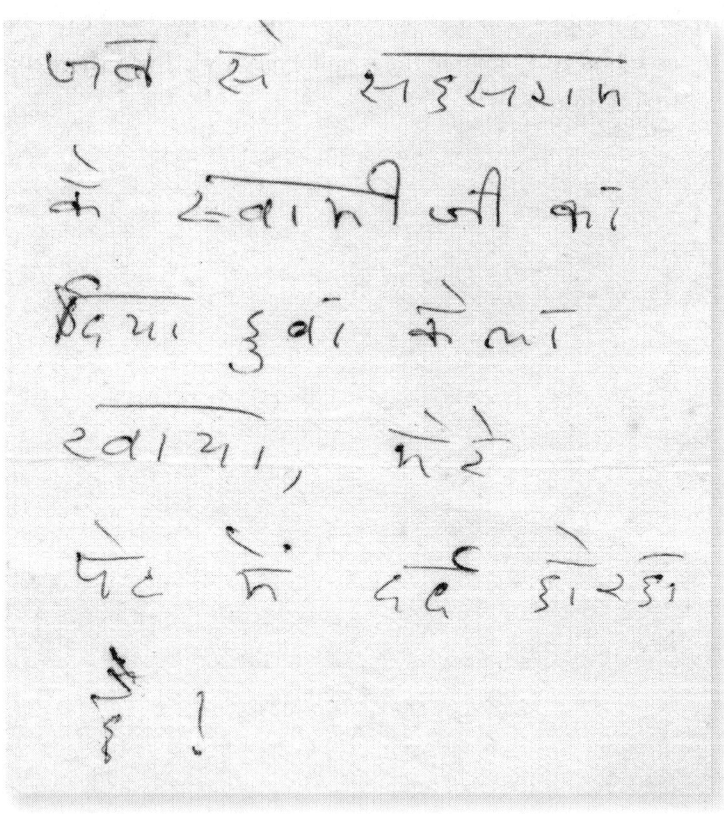

जब से सहसराम
के स्वामी जी का
दिया हुआ केला
खाया, मेरे
पेट में दर्द हो रहा
है!

NOTE 7 PM had once paid a visit to a famous baba in UP called Sasaram Baba. Her stomach started hurting after she partook of the *prasad*, a banana he had given her. Here, she rues that she ate it.

OTHER FAMILY MEMBERS

PM seemed to have a slight tilt towards her mother's family. She would often talk about her maternal uncles and a maternal aunt, Sheila Kaul, was one of the frequent visitors. Her cousins on the maternal side, Gautam and Naresh, who were stationed in Delhi, would also visit her quite often. Naresh Katju was a friend of Rajiv's and they shared many interests like running a ham radio club and he was often seen at PM's dining table. Gautam Kaul, Sheilaji's son, is a police officer. He used to be preoccupied with his own affairs yet would often call on PM.

Naresh's father, P.N. Katju, was PM's *mausa* (maternal uncle) and was a professor in Agra College; he later shifted to Jaipur from where he was elected as a member of Rajya Sabha and came to live in Delhi. PM was particularly attached to her *masi* (maternal aunt), Mrs Katju; any trip to Jaipur was not complete without PM meeting her.

P.N. Katju was a talkative person and PM had no time for his small talk. Mr Katju had been my chemistry teacher in Agra College and was quite popular those days with the boys for his nationalistic views; he preferred to wear an *achkan* with *churidar* and a Gandhi *topi* whereas other teachers were clad in suit and tie and wore solar hats.

To save herself from listening to Mr Katju's long stories, she would pass him on to me since I already knew him well, to face the music. But once when Mr Katju sustained a serious head injury, PM immediately sent for me to go and see him and report back immediately.

In his case, hospitalization for neurosurgical intervention was called for. I organized all that was necessary and she went to see him at AIIMS a couple of times. On another occasion, she took me to see one of her maternal uncles at his residence. The old man was sitting on the bed and appeared quite uncomfortable. His wife asked me if I was going to examine him and was quite satisfied when I proceeded to do so. I prescribed some medicines different to the ones he was already taking.

The elderly couple felt very happy and obliged to PM and me for having taken the trouble to see them. When offered, I declined my professional fee, as she was elder to me and even to PM; instead, I sought her blessings. Perhaps impressed by my humility and respect, the lady immediately stretched her hand out and placed it on mine and PM's head.

With her aunt, Vijayalakshmi Pandit, PM had an uneasy relationship. Mrs Pandit did not spare even her brother, Panditji. On one occasion, when she was staying with Panditji at Teen Murti House, I was called to see her for some minor ailment; I was yet to join Indira Gandhi as her personal physician. I prescribed her the medicine but she asked me to see her again the next morning. When I went to see her at the appointed time, she was not at home. I waited for her in the PA's room hoping that when she returned, somebody would inform me. She came back but obviously there was some lack of communication and I was not informed of her arrival. I kept waiting and after about an hour, I tried to find out what was happening. When I was ultimately called in, I received a dressing down. After I explained my position, in order to placate me, she came out with her explanation, "*Bhaiya*, this is not a home, but the devil's haunt!"

On another occasion when I was a little late in locating the place where she was staying, I was again the recipient of her comments, "What sort of a doctor are you? Being so late, in the meantime were the patient to die," she harangued.

During the General Elections of 1977, she left PM's side and joined Jagjivan Ram and others in the new party they had formed, the Congress for Democracy.

One person for whom PM had a very special regard was B.K. Nehru and his wife, Fori. Mr Nehru was one of the most distinguished civil servants, a man of unimpeachable integrity and PM admired his principles and propriety. Fori Nehru was a very interesting person, quite informal in her dealings. She used to crack a lot of jokes. She was also fond of narrating anecdotes of which she had quite a collection, thanks to her hectic diplomatic life. She could speak fluent Hindustani and chose to speak in it, using English words only when she could not find a Hindi equivalent.

PM was a loving mother, grand-mother and an understanding and non-interfering mother-in-law. She had great love and affection for both her sons though there was a slight change in her attitude during the Emergency period and thereafter, till Sanjay's death.

In her relationship with her two daughters-in-law there was an element of reciprocity. Although PM was always more fond of Sonia, during the period after Sanjay's death, she became a little more inclined towards Maneka. However, it failed to bring Maneka closer to her. Generally, Sonia held the upper hand in household affairs while Maneka's views were considered by PM when it came to political matters since Maneka had good political sense.

PM was especially affectionate towards Rahul and Priyanka. Every morning both of them would come to take leave of her before going to school; she would enquire what they had for breakfast or if they were carrying something to eat during the recess. She took particular interest in their education, including deciding upon which school they should be sent to. The children had already started going to Modern School in Delhi. Her friend, Pupul Jayakar, advised her to send the children to Rishi Valley School, Madanapally in Andhra Pradesh, started by the famous theosophist J. Krishnamurthy. I went with her to have a look at the place. However, in the end, PM decided that the children should be sent to Doon School.

Her affection did not stand in the way of the children maintaining discipline. Once, after they had joined school in Dehra Dun and were not able to come to Delhi to celebrate Diwali with the family, she herself went to Dehra Dun; the children were sent to PM's camp to celebrate Diwali.

According to school regulations, they were allowed to come only for a few hours and to return by a fixed time, which was quite early in the evening. We all celebrated Diwali before it was dark and had an early dinner so that the children could go back and PM gave special instructions to the security officer who accompanied them to hand over the children to the house master. The school regulations had been observed strictly, so no one could say that PM's grandchildren were being accorded any special treatment.

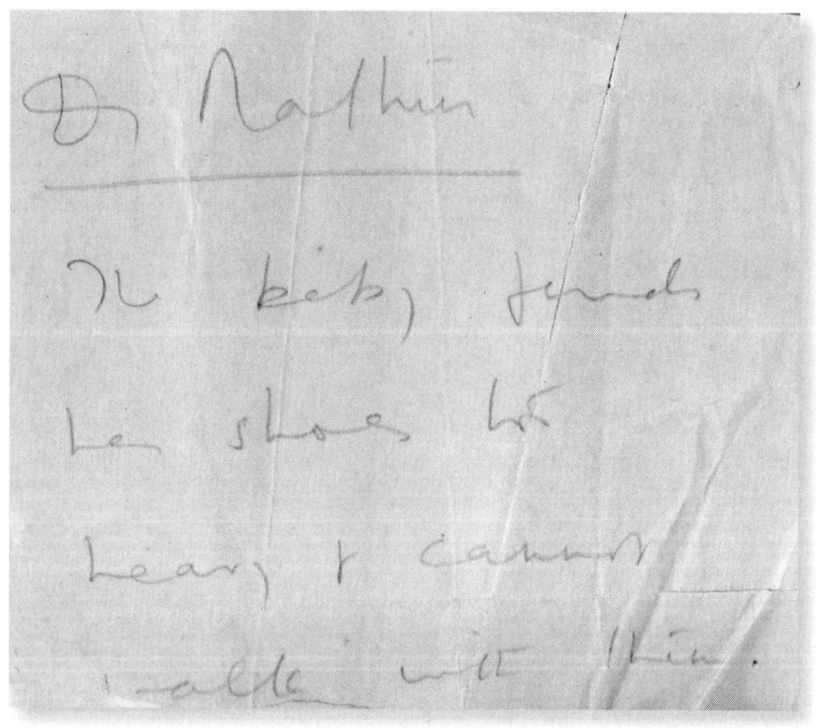
Dr Nathan

The baby finds her shoes too heavy & cannot walk with them.

NOTE 8 Priyanka Gandhi had a bit of a problem with her feet as a kid, so I got her custom made shoes that would be more comfortable for her but they turned out a little heavy. PM wrote to me saying that she cannot walk in her shoes because they are too heavy.

A LOVELY COUPLE

Sonia and Rajiv met each other when they were both studying at Cambridge and became friends; it seems it was love at first sight and very soon, they decided to get married. When Rajiv mentioned this to PM, she did not disagree but perhaps wanted some more time to take a final decision. She met Sonia a couple of times in England and approved of the match but the actual marriage had to wait because Sonia was a little under-age. Sonia came to Delhi a couple of days before the day of her wedding. In a TGV interview later on, she narrated that her father had given her a return ticket to come back home in case she did not find conditions in India and at home congenial and to her liking. Nothing of this sort happened and Rajiv and Sonia got married in Delhi on February 25, 1968. In the same interview, Sonia offered to give her return ticket to anyone who could make good use of it.

It was a quiet marriage ceremony at PM's house and very few people were invited for the actual wedding. But an elaborate reception was held in celebration of Rajiv and Sonia's wedding the next day at Hyderabad House. On the day of the reception, that is, the day after the marriage, PM sent for me early afternoon and asked me to check on Sonia who was lying in bed with a severe pain in the stomach. On examination, I found that she was struck with appendicitis. There was a reception for her within a few hours. I gave her some medicines and a couple of injections. She showed remarkable forbearance and patience; although still in pain, she stood by the two hours of reception without anyone noticing what she was undergoing.

PM and Sonia took to each other in no time. Sonia gave a lot of respect and the latter showered her with affection and regard. A couple of times in my presence, the cook and other servants came to PM for orders for the day and she referred them to *bahuraniji* (daughter-in-law). Sonia very soon took over the responsibility of running the household.

As for Rajiv, he was extremely handsome, amiable, soft-spoken and helpful, a lovable person in every respect. Later, even when he became the prime minister, he did not hesitate to open the bonnet of my car to fix something which had gone wrong. His hands were black with soot and grease afterwards and he had to wash them with kerosene or petrol.

Rajiv always greeted me with a smile and never forgot to exchange pleasantries. He also liked to discuss political gossip with me. One could really discuss anything under the sun with him.

One day, I had to go and meet him in the small hours of the morning (4 am) during election time. He was busy deciding about distribution of the tickets; and there were so many aspirants waiting to see him.

When my turn came, he came out himself and took me in. He was hungry not having eaten anything the whole day, so busy was he with the election work. He took a piece of fish and offered some to me.

"What! Fish at 4 a.m.; so early in the morning!" I wondered. Then he went inside the kitchen, searched for a bottle opener and served me a bottle of Coca-Cola. Such was his courtesy and amiability.

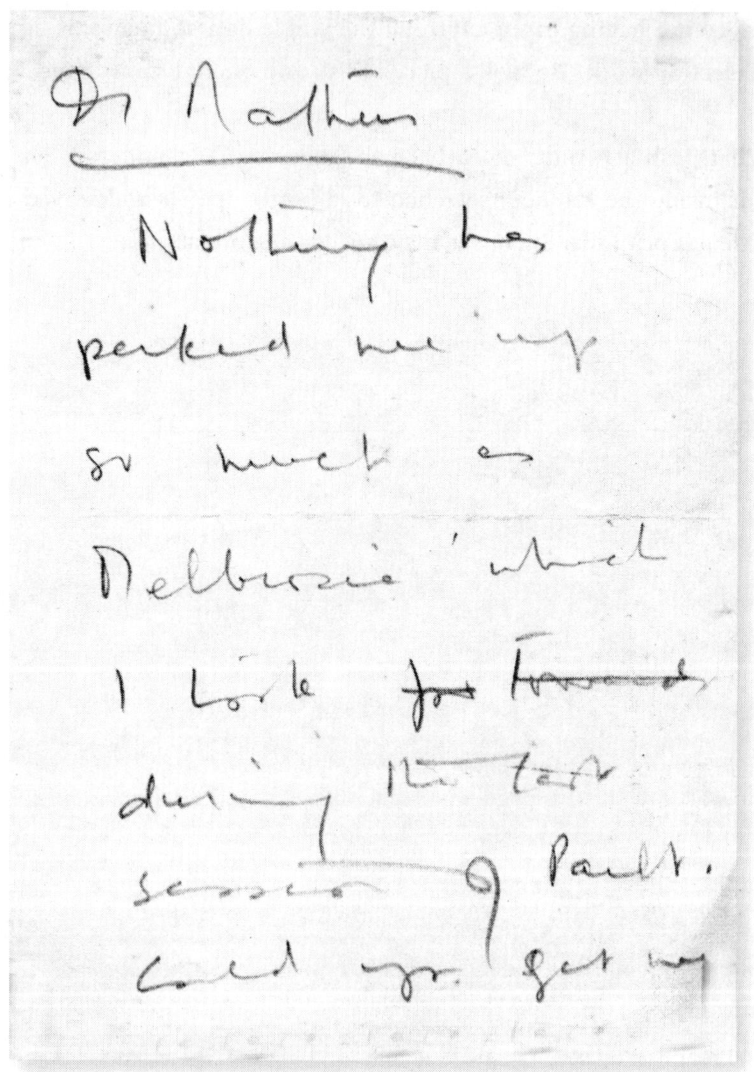

Dr Nathan

Nothing has
perked me up
so much as
Melbrosia which
I took for ~~[illegible]~~
during the last
session of Parlt.
Could you get me

NOTE 9 Here, PM says that nothing had perked her up as much as the Melbrosia which she took during the last session of the Parliament and if I could get her some more of it.

HOLIDAY SCHEDULES

PM's daily schedule used to be so busy and exacting that she hardly had any time to relax. On Sundays or other holidays, she relaxed with some books, especially biographies of great men. She also liked to read books on subjects connected with the body and mind as well as popular science magazines. She was fond of solving crossword puzzles in international publications like *Life, The Times* and *Newsweek*, among others to keep herself fully informed. Once, she told me that she found herself feeling relaxed while applying her mind to something difficult and more demanding than the daily run of the mill things.

These would be the days when she would order her meals, which would always be something different from the everyday menu that other family members decided upon. On such days, she would put on different kind of dresses: Sikkimese gowns, African kaftans or Japanese kimonos. On some free days, she liked to wear a saree in the Bengali style or even the salwar-kameez. Some friends like Pupul Jayakar would call on her on days like these and share a meal.

During the earlier days of her premiership, Indira Gandhi would go for holidays for a change or some rest or to catch up with her reading. As time went by, she had so much to do that there was not much time left for such luxuries.

In those days, when she could afford them, her favourite place for holidays was Kashmir. Making Srinagar her base, she would take short trips to neighbouring places of interest.

From day one, a routine was drawn up to ensure maximum economy and to minimize any burden on state hospitality. A menu would be drawn up which was kept as simple as possible. It was generally vegetarian food, but sometimes some well flavoured Kashmiri non-vegetarian dishes were also included. We all were expected to tidy our rooms, make the beds, and clean our bathrooms, share our cars, etc. All of us had to sit down for meals together in the dining room so that we could make do with just a few servants. PM's favourite haunt in Kashmir was Dachi Gam, an old hunting lodge of the Maharajas, a beautifully constructed old style country house decorated with pictures of animals and other photographs of early Maharajas in their shooting kit and guns and their prize catches. All rooms were fully carpeted and wood-panelled to keep them warm and comfortable. A fireplace in the old style used to be in all rooms. Later, central heating came into vogue, and the old world charm of fireplaces was largely given up.

Sometimes, after lunch, she liked to play cards. Her favourite card game was Kali Mam which none of us knew how to play. On one occasion, she engaged us in play-acting. On small chits of paper the acts which were to be performed by each person were noted.

These chits were then put in a large jar from which each one was asked to pick up one chit and act the role indicated. Yashpal Kapoor, her PA, picked up a chit on which was written *sapera* (snake charmer).

Kapoor made some clumsy movements with one hand flexing his wrist making a sideways movement like a snake in the basket. He moved the other hand in front of his chest up and down like a *sapera* (snake charmer) playing his *been* (snake charmer's flute). Everyone had a good laugh and enjoyed Kapoor's histrionics. On my turn as noted in my chit, I had to play "the Arab sheikh of oil and gas". Those were the days of the international oil crisis and newspapers were full of it, which was, perhaps, on her mind too. It was a pretty difficult part to play in comparison with others who had to play simpler or commonplace roles. Without looking nervous, I wrapped a towel lying there round my head to look like an Arab's headgear, I pulled out a bed-sheet and wrapped it around my body to resemble the Arab gown called "Thob" and caught hold of an empty bottle of Coca-Cola lying there to make for a bottle of crude oil.

With small steps, I walked forward making a hissing noise with my lips, like gas leaking from an oil well. Everyone had a hearty laugh and PM also appeared to enjoy my acting.

Pointing toward me, she made an announcement, "Look, when I retire from active political life, I will start a theatre company and I would employ you as one of my lead actors." But alas, she did not live to get her retirement, neither was the theatre company started nor did I become the lead actor.

During one such visit, PM returned to Dachi Gam around dusk one day after finishing her day's work. It was getting dark. Officers on duty at Dachi Gam, having finished their duty, wanted to go to their homes in Srinagar.

Immediately on arrival, PM decided that she would like to visit a small forest area not far from Dachi Gam, where the maharaja had kept a wildlife preserve. A motor convoy was quickly put in place for PM's visit, but there was also a sizable convoy of officers going back to Srinagar after their duties. The somewhat large scale and sudden movement of cars created much noise, dust and din. The animals had already returned to their resting places. All this resulted in PM not being able to see any animals. The lion, like other royalty, was also protocol-conscious and did not come out to meet a mere Prime Minister. PM had to return disappointed and angry. She thought that the animals' refusal to come out was the result of fright caused by the noise and dust raised by the motor convoys. In a flash of temper and without waiting for any explanation, she ordered that henceforth no other cars, even security cars, would follow her. She would like to go all by herself. She particularly ordered that neither the doctor, nor the PA or any other officers were to follow her. Her orders were final and appeared irrevocable. Hearing this, the security staff was very upset, as they were likely to be questioned by their superiors if they let PM go by herself. But luckily, Rajiv had come with PM on this tour and the security officers went up to him on bent knees, begging forgiveness. Rajiv succeeded in placating PM but only partially; PM reluctantly agreed to allow one or two security cars to follow her but no other member of the staff could come, including the doctor. I was virtually grounded and felt helpless under the circumstances.

Incidentally, a few days later PM was to tour Tanzania which is famous for its wildlife. No programme in that country could be complete without a visit to see the wildlife. A programme for such a visit had already been fixed and organized by our embassy there.

Mr Bansi Lal was the minister-in-waiting during this visit and was to accompany PM on this excursion. I did not know what to do and stood at the door of the palace where we were staying. My call of duty demanded that I follow PM, but her orders were quite clear.

Bansi Lal saw my quandary and asked me the reason for it. After hearing me out, he pulled me inside his car. PM saw me and pointing a finger, said, "What are you doing here?" Before I could answer her, Bansi Lal said, "Behenji, it is all right that you do not need a doctor, but who knows a lion might get injured or hurt somewhere and needs the services of a doctor who would at least give first aid and bandage the wounds." Everyone had a good laugh at the repartee. Bansi Lal's rustic humour saved the day for me. The matter was finished and no one ever raised it again.

Bansi Lal as Chief Minister of Haryana did many things and one of them was to develop a resort on Badhkal Lake near Gurgaon. This was an ambitious programme but his heart was set on it. When it was about to finish and ready, he thought it should be inaugurated by PM on her birthday and spoke to her about this. PM agreed for the inauguration but on one condition, that her visit be kept a closely guarded secret. We drove down a day earlier in the evening and reached Badhkal around dark. We were lodged in cottages that had been recently constructed. When I went to the room assigned to me, I found that apart from the usual furniture and fittings, a copy of the Quran Sharif was placed on the table in the centre of the room. This was a little surprising. After some time, I went to see PM and I saw the Quran Sharif there too. PM expressed her surprise as well and was curious to know the reason behind it.

After an hour or so, my friend S.K. Mishra, the Director General, Tourism, Haryana, came to see me. He was also in-charge of all the arrangements and I asked him about the mystery. At first, he laughed it away but then told me that since this visit was a secret, the hurried arrangements were causing curiosity among all the workers; and for their satisfaction it was let out that a very wealthy Arab sheikh was coming and these arrangements were being made for him. When I mentioned this to PM, she also laughed and said a few words of praise for Mishra's ingenuity.

MEMORANDUM.

Dr. Mathur –

As you know I have to wear glasses in the morning & in the evening. The evening tension of the eyes has been tested but is it also necessary to test the morning tension? The President thinks so & has advised me accordingly.

IG.

Several eye checks performed on P.M. so far have been unrewarding. I wonder if she would consider submitting herself to another one at the hands of one of the specialists of the Moorfield hospital when P.M. goes to London.

P.M.

K P Mathur
24.12.68

NOTE 10 PM had some trouble with her eyes and complained that they kept watering so I suggested that she go to Moorefield Hospital in London when she is in London next which was famous for treating diseases of the eye.

SATURDAY EPISODES

For quite some time, I had made it a practice to see PM every Saturday early in the morning between 7 and 7.30. At that time, she was fully rested and completely relaxed and also had some time to answer my queries as to how she had been all through the week. Normally, she was reticent and did not like to talk much about her health problems. She had no patience to narrate her symptoms or allow for any clinical examination. In fact, one day when persuaded and in good humour, she told me: "Look, I don't need a physician; I want a vet who would not ask any questions or ask for any examination; one look and everything should be done."

On Saturdays, the routine was that I would go to PM's house at the appointed time and reported to Nathu Ram, her valet who would know whether PM was awake, because he was the first person to see her in the morning. Nathu Ram would then accompany me to PM's door. A knock and the response would be "come in" or "*aaiye*" and I would go in.

After exchanging pleasantries, I would ask her how she had been feeling. A brief clinical examination would follow: blood pressure, tongue, nails for anaemia, heart and lungs and it would be over. I would go and wait in the next room in case she would like to say something. In the meantime, PM would get ready for breakfast and her day's work would start.

Some tea, coffee and something to eat would be brought by the servant for me. Once, it so happened that a day earlier, someone had brought *sarda* (a melon) for her from Afghanishtan. She asked the servant to get some *sarda* for me too. It was really sweet and juicy and I relished it.

PM was very particular that nothing should be wasted, especially the edibles. The *sarda* was a big one and PM also saw that I liked it so a slice or two were brought for me every morning whenever I went to see her. One day, I was in a hurry and the servant was also a little slow in getting the *sarda* for me. I left but right then, the man came running after me, "Dr Sa'ab, please come and take your *sarda*." I had to go back and finish my share for the day.

Most Saturdays were routine affairs but sometimes, these could be quite interesting and even amusing. On one Saturday morning, as I entered PM's room, she confronted me by asking in a peculiar bantering manner why I was conspiring against a certain Dr Shree Ram*. I was taken aback; the previous evening I had learnt that Dr Shree Ram was trying to grab a post in the Lohia Hospital which rightfully belonged to one Dr Mehta; all sorts of pulls and pressures were being applied and even PM had been approached. She had also been wrongly informed that I was trying to prevent him from getting the post. When PM questioned me about the *shadyantra* (conspiracy), I could immediately guess which Dr Shree Ram it was. But even then, I asked her, "Who is this Shree Ram?"

* Names have been changed here.

She responded, "How do I know? You are the one who is doing all this *shadyantra* and you are asking me who is Shree Ram?" She said all this in a lighter vein. I felt reassured with her way of talking and explained to her the whole truth. I added that if Shree Ram were to get the post, it would be very unfair towards Dr Mehta who was the rightful claimant for this position. I stopped at that and waited for her response. Carrying on in the same light vein and laughing at my discomfort, she again talked of *shadyantra*, saying, "You do what you like, I am not in it". Later, I tried to find out how the matter reached PM and learnt that an MP with whom Dr Shree Ram was friendly had spoken to PM and also complained about me.

After a couple of days, Dr Mehta, and not Dr Shree Ram, got the appointment letter for the post. Justice done, manipulation failed.

One Saturday morning when I went to see her, I saw her looking at an invitation card for a wedding that was to be held in a hotel. Obviously it was a day-long affair as it is generally these days. She became nostalgic about the wedding celebrations and the gaiety during weddings in her younger days while expressing her dismay about their current avatar. She went on to narrate in detail about the weddings; I listened to her patiently. "In our families," she recalled, "weddings were generally were at least three or four day affairs. Close relations would arrive several days earlier. Somebody would be awarded the contract for victuals, fruits, and meats etc. Special cooks would be commissioned from Srinagar to prepare well-flavoured Kashmiri cuisine. The best of local *halwais* were called and so on. She elaborated by saying that these days, it was more like planning a conference.

I responded by saying that elaborate and lengthy weddings held at homes were possible due to the blessings of the joint family system. Such weddings, alas, could not be organized anymore and people had to fall back on hotels. I also told her that the joint family system was not all that good as she had described it and that there were some less than savoury aspects to it.

The conversation now moved to the increasing number of failed marriages, separations and divorces happening these days. She remained mostly taciturn about the topic but said, "I know of only two marriages which are happy." A little surprised at this low figure I asked her, "Ma'am, if you could say who they were, we could learn from them and make our lives happier." She laughed and said, "forget it; it is too late in life for you to learn anything now." A couple of days later, I narrated the incident to one of her lady secretaries, her close confidant, to know who these two lucky couples were. She replied that she was also not sure who they were, but named two which she thought PM might be referring to. They were B.K. Nehru and Fori Nehru, and Rajiv and Sonia.

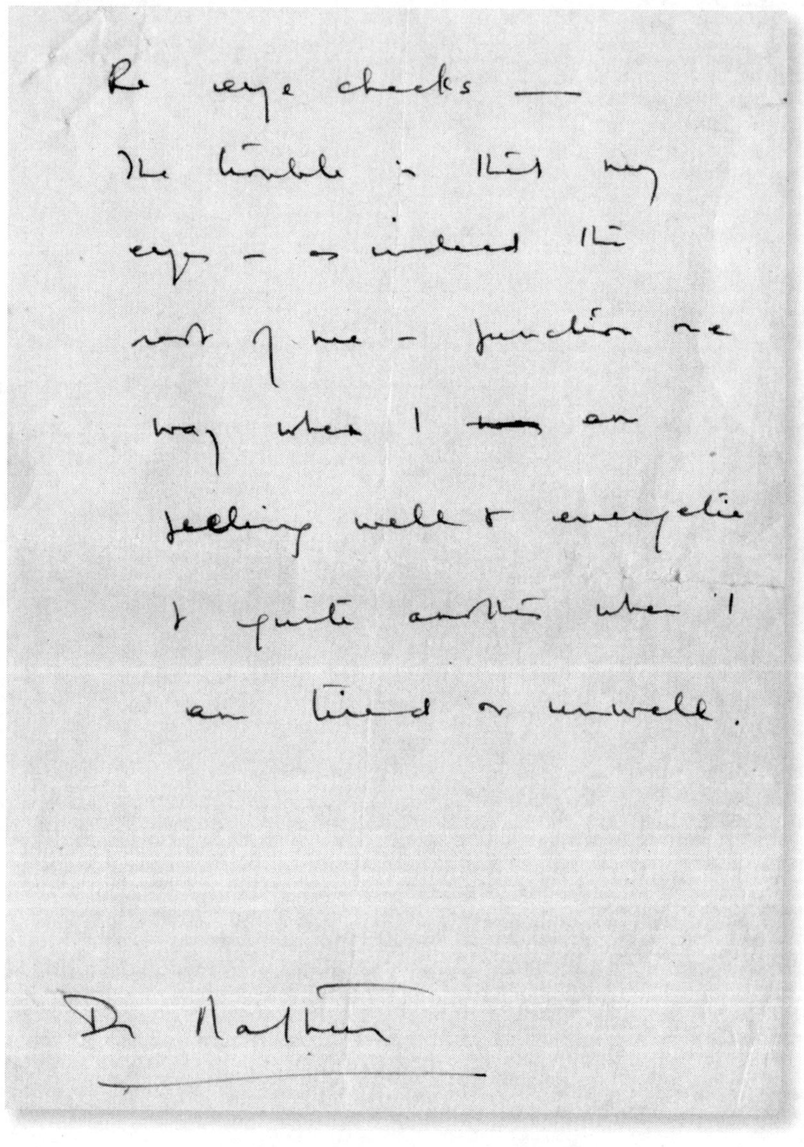

Re eye checks —

The trouble is that my eyes – as indeed the rest of me – function one way when I am feeling well & energetic & quite another when I am tired or unwell.

Dr Nathan

NOTE 11 The eye check saga was put to rest when PM wrote that her eyes troubled her only when she was tired and did not need any medical intervention.

FIRST STEPS AT THE HELM

The Congress still had popular support but it had to face criticism for its faulty policies that led to the Chinese incursion. It was natural that such failure beget criticism.

The years before Indira Gandhi took over as PM were quite turbulent, starting with the Sino-Indian war and another one with Pakistan soon after, in 1965 although life went on normally for the most part.

Indira Gandhi took over as PM in 1966, after the death of Lal Bahadur Shastri in Tashkent, the capital of Uzbekistan, where he had gone to hammer out an agreement with his Pakistani counterpart, General Ayub Khan, following the war in 1965.

During the first year or two of her becoming PM, she used to be very tense, a bit confused and not sure of herself. She had no advisors and was almost friendless. Before she became PM, during her tenure as the president of the Congress Party and thereafter as Minister in Shastriji's cabinet, she had friends who became her close advisors and were often referred to as the "kitchen cabinet". However, after she became Prime Minister, she did not always follow their advice. The "kitchen cabinet", comprising of Dinesh Singh, Inder Gujral, Ramesh Thapar and others, became superfluous and got dissolved. Only Dinesh Singh stayed on as an advisor and friend.

Many of those who helped her become a prime minister and wanted to be put on a pedestal found themselves on the shelf. Their dream was for PM to reign but for themselves to rule.

TTK and Krishna Menon were openly her critics. I was close to both of them.

Once, I overheard TTK advise someone when the latter mentioned his difficulty in obtaining an appointment to see PM. "It is very easy", he had said and added that all that he had to do was to approach Dinesh Singh and his work will be done.

Krishna Menon used to make fun of me but the target of his jokes was PM.

Once while introducing me to a friend of his, he described me as a man from the palace; meet "Dr Mathur, the famous paediatrician". The man somewhat knew me and was aware that I was a physician and not a paediatrician. He asked, "What is a paediatrician doing in PM's house?" Both had a good laugh at the pun.

In the initial phase of her premiership, PM used to be especially nervous, when faced with some speaking assignments, either in Parliament or outside and would try to avoid it.

For example, in 1969, she had to present the budget, as she had taken over the finance portfolio from Morarji Desai. I had gone to see her in the morning on the day she was scheduled to present it and she was quite nervous, and was speaking in whispers.

I knew it was nervousness, still I tried to help her recover her voice by suggesting gargling and some sprays but nothing seemed to help. I even consulted a couple of other doctors. But they were also unable to help as the malady was really in her mind. I was worried that if she could not present the budget, I would be blamed for not being able to cure her.

However, at the end of it, she made a fine speech in Parliament and presented the budget successfully.

She would also get stomach upsets in the early days of being PM which I believe was the result of the same nervousness. After all, it is said that the stomach is the springboard of all emotions.

I remember on one occasion, she had to go for electioneering in Kerala while she had an upset stomach. I tried to stop her but she was insistent. She had to cover 300 miles in a day and we had to make sure that every government building that fell on the way would be ready for PM's to use, if necessary. However, in the end, these were not required.

Notwithstanding the initial jitters, she was a very determined person. The riots in Tamil Nadu over making Hindi the national language were still not quelled when she took over as PM and that state was its epicenter. (In 1965, the 15-year deadline to make Hindi the national language came to an end and the Central Government clamped down on the protestors and it is cited as the prime reason behind the Congress' defeat in the 1967 elections in the state. The party never returned to power in Tamil Nadu).

During that same tour when she visited Kerala, she was also scheduled to visit the Madras University. However, because of security reasons, she was advised not to go there. But she countered by saying, "One part of the country is on fire. How can I not go there?"

She did visit the Madras University which was the epicenter of the anti-Hindi protests and addressed the students, remaining undaunted by their hostile sloganeering. She told the students, "Don't say down with Hindi. Say up with Tamil. I will learn Tamil and you also learn Hindi." Immediately, there were claps of approval and the situation was saved.

I could see her gaining in confidence with each passing day. This became visible to all when she caused a split in the Congress party and created her own faction, the Congress (R) in 1969. This was a blow to the old guard led by Morarji Desai, then deputy PM, who led the faction called Congress (O). Desai finally joined the Janata Party and became PM after Emergency was lifted. I knew Moraji Desai but not very well. He was always guarded in conversation with me as I was considered to be an "Indira man". However, he did advise me once to prescribe urine therapy to my patients which he was very fond of. I never did that but I listened to his suggestion with humility as I did not want to offend him by telling him I did not agree with his suggestion.

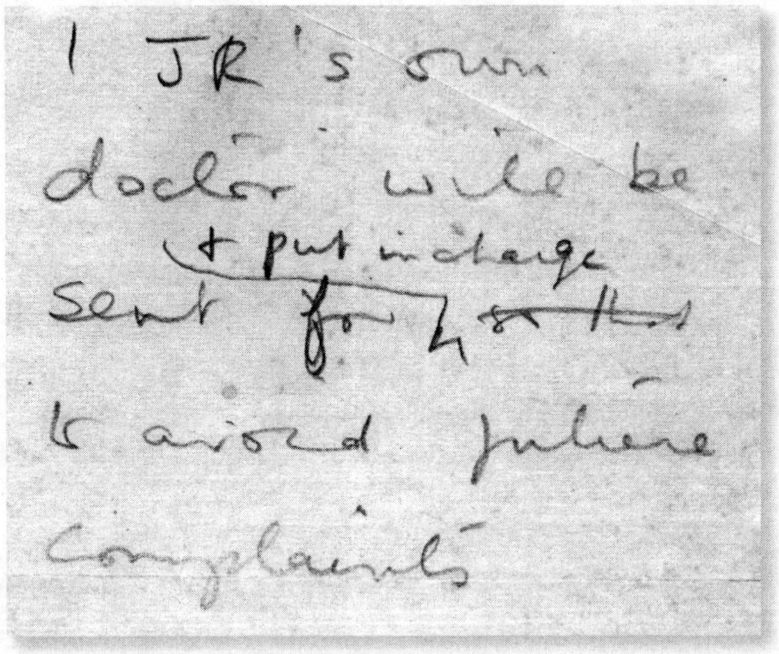

1 JR's own
doctor will be
& put in charge
sent for
to avoid future
complaints

NOTE 12 Jagjivan Ram was coming to Delhi for his treatment for asthma. He was to be admitted to Ram Manohar Lohia Hospital. PM recommended that his own doctor be put in charge to avoid future complaints. I think she did this to do away with the possibility of any political games.

BANGLADESH FACE-OFF

As is well known, Pakistan was formed by carving out Muslim majority areas out of the original undivided India. This resulted in two big regions, one in India's East and the other in the West, separated from each other by a distance of 1200 km. Except for their religious identity, there was nothing in common between the two halves of Pakistan. Physically, culturally, linguistically and emotionally they were like chalk and cheese. Their dress is different as also the language. One can go on listing the differences between the two and therefore, it was not surprising that they could not remain together for long. Religion alone was not an adhesive strong enough to keep them united. West Pakistanis looked upon their Bengali brethren with contempt. They thought the Bengalis whom they derisively called Bingos were physically weak and culturally inferior. West Pakistanis were undoubtedly physically strong. They considered Bengal as a colony; and its natural resources were exploited by West Pakistan without any benefits accruing to East Pakistan. What hurt the Bengalis most was that their language was not recognized by the Central Pakistan Government. The army was totally made up of Punjabis and Pathans; and the best jobs also went to those from West Pakistan. The military regime in power that ruled both the halves also suited the interests of West Pakistan as it included primarily those living there.

In December 1970, polls were held to bring a democratic regime to power in which Sheikh Mujibur Rahman and his party scored a thundering victory. Mujibur Rahman was the leader of the Awami League. He was fiercely patriotic and a great orator in Bengali; he was well-loved by the people of Bangladesh who considered him their supreme leader. Despite such a convincing majority, the West Pakistanis refused to accept him as their Prime Minister and did everything to make it impossible for the electoral verdict to be implemented. They tried to harass the Bengalis in every possible way, making their lives miserable. This led to the rise of a national movement for the liberation of East Pakistan under the leadership of Sheikh Mujibur Rahman.

Instead of doing something to assuage the feelings of their Bengali brethren, they unleashed a reign of terror and put Mujibur Rahman in jail. To subdue the Bengalis, they even sent their army. Frustrated Bengali youth were organizing themselves into a liberation army. Humiliated, terrorized, and deprived in every way, these youths ran across the border into adjoining Indian states like Assam and Tripura, among others. The number of such refugees coming to India every day was increasing rapidly, causing major problems. To feed them, clothe them and provide them shelter soon became a stupendous task for the people and the government. The local state governments were not able to deal with the situation and sought help from the Centre. PM took the situation in hand, and made a number of trips to Assam, Tripura and other places where the bulk of these refugees had crossed over for food and shelter. PM could speak Bengali; thus she could converse with the refugees and understand their problems. Finding a sympathetic ear, the hapless refugees narrated their tales of woe. With tears in their eyes, the women narrated in detail how they had been molested by the West Pakistani army personnel in *mufti* (civilian clothes), hiding their identity. After hearing them, at one stage, PM had tears in her eyes also. India went all out to help these people in distress. PM decided to go the whole hog to assist in their liberation movement by supporting the Mukti Bahini and in other ways.

A Bangladesh government-in-exile was formed in India. The turmoil in Bengal had created problems for India and whole of South East Asia. What was happening in East Bengal amounted to suppression of the legitimate aspirations of a people. PM also appealed to the conscience of the world to solve this problem.

She undertook a tour to some Western countries, including England, USA, France, West Germany and the Soviet Union. The news about the atrocities committed on the East Bengalis aroused great sympathy all over the world. I accompanied her on these tours. Other than the leaders of these countries, she met a number of prominent personalities, including intellectuals and was able to arouse their sympathy for the Bengali cause.

The impatient regime in West Pakistan started the war on December 3, 1971 by conducting simultaneous air strikes on many Indian air bases in Punjab and other places, leading to India's entry into the war for the liberation of East Pakistan, on the side of Bangladeshi nationalist forces, and the commencement of hostilities with West Pakistan. PM was informed of the air strikes and that Pakistan had declared a war while she was addressing a public meeting in Calcutta. She started her speech with "*Aami Bangla bujhte pari, bolte pari na*" (I can understand Bangla but I can't speak it) immediately endearing herself to the crowd.

She immediately returned to Delhi. During the flight, she was cool and composed as ever; her mind was obviously occupied with strategy of war, the future course of action and also the announcement she was due to make on radio that night.

Security cover was provided by the Air Force when we landed in Delhi; there was a complete blackout. PM went to her office to hold a meeting of the Cabinet to decide upon the future course of action. She also made a special broadcast to the nation. Her speech was prepared by her Press Advisor H.Y. Sharada Prasad. Completely unruffled by the events, she sat in her office till well past midnight. I just thought it my duty that I should be with her and stay in PM's house for the night, just in case of any emergency. PM absolutely disapproved of that, and instead, asked me to go straight home and be with my family who might also be scared by the sudden turn of events: the war and blackout. After delivering her instruction PM went out of the house for the broadcast. I took her valet Nathuram into confidence and had a bed prepared for myself in another room in the house where I quietly spent the night. In the early hours of the next morning, I went to my house and after attending to the morning chores, I was back at PM's house as was my practice every day. I found her spreading a new sheet on the diwan in her office room. She was quite composed and in good cheer as if nothing untoward had happened. She asked me with a smile if I slept well at night, unaware that I was in her own house the whole night.

As the war progressed, there were daily discussions between PM, the Commander-in-Chief, General Sam Manekshaw, the Defence Minister and other senior officers of Defence Ministry. General Manekshaw assured PM that the war would not last long. The war effectively came to an end, in the East, by the act of Pakistani surrender on December 16, and in the West—of our own accord—by cease-fire.

Bangladesh had been liberated and there was rejoicing all round the country. PM had reached the highest point of her political career. Tributes were paid to her for the courage, strength and determination she showed; even the Opposition was showering fullsome praise on her with Atal Bihari Vajpayeeji calling her "Durga" Ma while paying tribute to her in Parliament.

NOTE 13 PM had left her spectacles behind and had asked me to look for them. I asked her about the ones she had and if they were her own. To that, she said that those were Rajiv's and he had taken them with him and she doesn't remember what he had done with them.

THE SHIMLA SUMMIT

When the war was over and Bangladesh was liberated, the problems of the new nation were solved to a large extent, but the-long standing problems between India and Pakistan continued to fester. And some new ones were added. Among these one of the important ones was the rehabilitation of a few lakh refugees who had migrated illegally from Bangladesh and were staying in Assam and the North-Eastern States leading to the creation of strife and social unrest.

The great financial burden on India and the fate of about 90,000 prisoners of war was also at stake. To find some solution to these problems, a number of meetings were held between our officers and those of Pakistan but no conclusions could be reached. Therefore, to find a final solution it was decided that heads of both governments, Mr Zulfikar Ali Bhutto and Mrs Indira Gandhi, meet and take a final decision. This was the reason for holding what came to be known as the "Shimla Summit".

The Shimla Summit was held in the last week of June and the first week of July 1972, almost six months after the war. PM was very keen that all arrangements for the conference should be first class and that Mr Bhutto should be treated with the greatest courtesy and due consideration. She did not want to cause him any further humiliation by any action of our country since he had already been a humiliated person in the eyes of everybody, including his own countrymen.

Arrangements had been made for Mr Bhutto and the senior members of the Pakistani delegation to stay at Himachal Bhawan at Shimla. The other members of the delegations of both countries were to be put in different hotels, guest houses, etc. PM had always stayed at the Retreat, a small wooden cottage consisting of four to five bedrooms. During British rule, when the Capital used to shift from Delhi to Shimla, the Viceroy used to stay there. She liked the place as it was on top of a hill, quiet, far from the city and surrounded by the woods where she liked to take long walks. All arrangements had been made to make Mr Bhutto as comfortable and satisfied as possible. His favourite drinks, cigars, etc. had also been arranged. A day before the conference, PM and party reached Shimla by helicopter and landed at Annandale helipad. On the way to the Retreat, PM passed by the side of the Himachal Bhawan which was going to be Mr Bhutto's residence and stopped to have a look if all the arrangements were up to the mark. She was not quite satisfied with a few things and gave instructions based on which many things were changed; new upholstery, curtains, bed linen, and a new sofa set were brought in; she really looked into the smallest of details and nothing was left to chance. While leaving, she asked Usha Bhagat to keep an eye as well. Meanwhile, a policeman on duty inside the building started a running commentary on PM's movements "now the VIP has entered the kitchen; now she is checking the cushions and the sofas," till somebody stopped him and put some sense into his head. PM spent nearly half an hour there.

Next morning, the Pakistani delegation was to arrive. We woke up quite early and got ready and reached the Annandale helipad where Mr Bhutto and his party were due to land. Soon after, they arrived as expected which was followed by the usual introductions and handshakes. Since I was not a formal member of our delegation, the security officer and I were standing near PM's car waiting for them to arrive. As they approached, Mr Bhutto appeared a little nervous and tense, looking this way and that, and walking slowly a little behind PM. When they were near PM's car, the security officer opened the door and I quickly went to my car, which was a few paces behind. I could see Mr Bhutto waiting for a while to display etiquette and allow PM to get in first. PM gestured to Mr Bhutto to enter first. Nervous as he was, Mr Bhutto jumped into the car and squeezed himself in one corner of the back seat. PM followed and the security officer closed the door. The motorcade moved on. Mr Bhutto sat silently. Despite tight security, a good number of people had assembled on both sides of the road; but they were standing quietly. After a little while, I could see from my car PM putting her hand out from her car in front and waving to the crowd outside. Immediately, there was the usual clapping and slogan shouting as ever. The motorcade moved slowly. After we reached, Himachal Bhawan I went straight to the Retreat where we staying. Breakfast was ready. I quickly finished and browsed through the morning papers. After a few minutes, PM also arrived after dropping Mr Bhutto. She went straight to the dining room. She appeared a little tense and confused and depressed making gestures in the air and nodding her head absent-mindedly. She did not seem like her usual composed self. Seeing her thus, I went and sat on a chair near her table, which I often did on tours whenever I found PM taking her meals alone; she quite approved of it. We both were sitting quietly and in order to break the silence, I started some small talk. I complimented her on the morning's reception which had gone off quite well. She lit up upon hearing this and asked me if I also felt that Mr Bhutto seemed quite tense and nervous. I agreed. She further said that he sat quietly all the while in the car, hardly looking out once or twice.

According to PM, Mr Bhutto was not sure if the crowd waiting by the side of the road was to greet him or get at him. PM said she had to reassure him that they were there to greet him as he was a guest.

After she narrated about the trip in the car, we sat in silence for a while. Suddenly, she said that she was depressed and asked me to narrate a "nice joke."

Apparently, on the way Mr Bhutto had said something which had made PM doubtful about the outcome of the conference. I had been a "court" physician for a number of years but certainly not a jester, able to narrate a joke whenever asked for. Mindful of the teaching of my guru, General Maitra, the President's doctor, who had told me never to act smart when in the presence of VIPs but to play it cool, I kept quiet. Dr Maitra had been a doctor to the first President, Dr Rajendra Prasad, and later to another President, Dr S. Radhakrishnan.

After waiting for a few moments, PM got bored by the silence and made a signal with the tip of her index finger touching her thumb, signifying zero. It was her way of saying that I had failed to entertain her when she demanded it.

I took leave of her and left for my room where I received a a phone call from Mohammad Yunus. Yunus had been long-time friend of PM's family. He was a Pathan and a relative and the private secretary to Khan Abdul Ghaffar Khan, the Frontier Gandhi. He later joined the Foreign Service and served as ambassador to many countries.

He told me that Mr Bhutto's doctor had expressed a desire to meet PM's doctor. I agreed but went to PM first to seek her permission. PM immediately agreed and asked me to go and keep him company. Yunus had positioned himself in the Himachal Bhawan to make sure that everything went off well. Some senior members of the Pakistani delegation were his friends as they all belonged to the North-West Frontier Province.

I went to Himachal Bhawan to meet the doctor. I asked him the usual questions assuming it was his first visit to Shimla and which spots he would like to go to. It was his first trip, he conceded, and added that his wife used to come to Shimla every year during the annual shifting of the Government of India secretariat (during summer months) from Delhi during the British days. Apparently, she was very nostalgic and wanted to accompany her husband on this trip to Shimla which was obviously not possible as it was a strictly official trip. I suggested to the doctor that he take some photographs of important landmarks of Shimla and show them to his wife which would refresh her memories of the old days. The doctor also expressed his desire to meet a relative of his who lived in Shimla. The security officer volunteered that the place where his relative lived was close from where we were at that moment. He took the doctor there and back. By this time we had been out for nearly two hours and it was time for lunch. We went to the Himachal Bhawan where lunch was being laid out and, in due course, other Pakistani delegates also arrived for lunch. I noticed that most of the guests were ordering vegetarian food. A little surprised, I enquired of the doctor if there was any special reason for the this preference for vegetarian meal. The doctor explained that they get non-vegetarian food every day in their homes which is why they wanted to try out the vegetarian fare in India which is well known for it. Yunus intervened and explained to them that the meat being served to them was *halal* not *jhatka* in case that was the reason they were avoiding it. However, the Pakistanis ate both varieties of meals, vegetarian and non-vegetarian, with great relish.

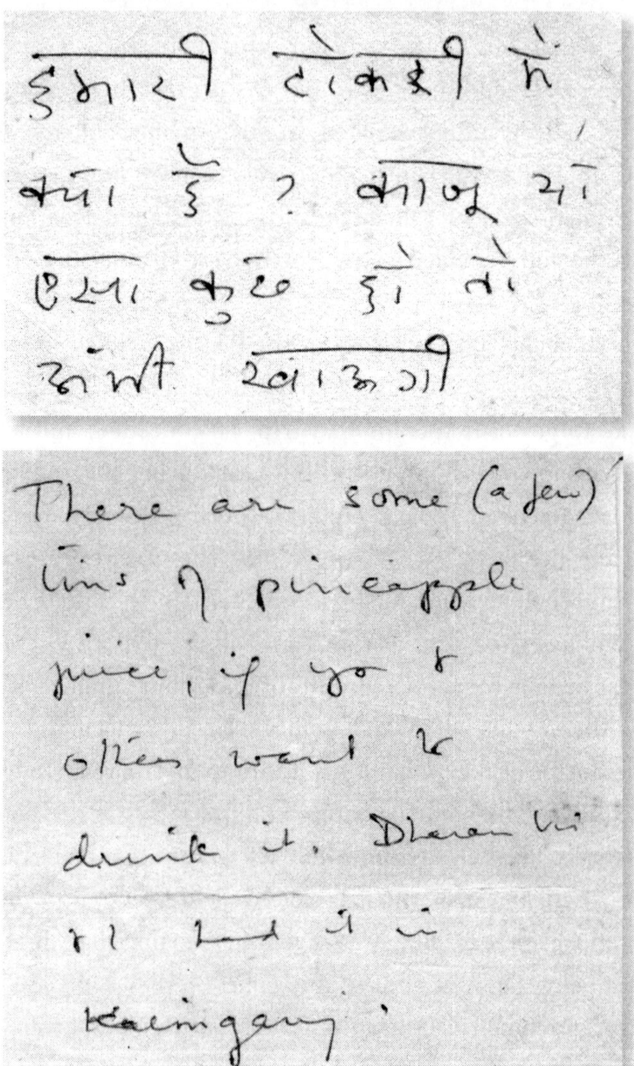

हमारी टोकरी में
क्या है? काजू या
ऐसा कुछ हो तो
अभी खाऊंगी

There are some (a few)
tins of pineapple
juice, if you &
others want to
drink it. Dhawan &
I had it in
Kaimganj.

NOTE 14 Once on a flight, she sent me a note asking what was in her snack basket. If there were cashews or something similar, only then would she eat them. Some time later, she sent another note saying there are some tins of pineapple juice, if I or the others, wanted, we could have them. Dhawan and she had them in Kaimganj.

BUDDHA'S SMILE AT POKHRAN

On May 18, 1974, that fateful Saturday morning when history was being made and the earth about to shake, I went to PM's house at about 7.30 and reported to Nathu Ram; however, instead of accompanying me to PM's door as he always did, he merely signalled with his hands as if to say "you can go, she is awake, the door is open."

I found the door ajar; I knocked and PM responded as usual, with the "*aaiye*, please come in". Hesitatingly, I went inside and to my surprise, PM was fully and formally dressed and ready for the day, sitting on her bed, and looking into some papers, not attentive towards me. My greetings were acknowledged reluctantly but no word of welcome was uttered which was unusual; I was not even asked to sit down. PM appeared to be under some strain or a little confused as she looked this way and that. She would sometimes get up and pick up the phone and put it down. She appeared quite perplexed and fidgety. When I asked about her health, she just answered in monosyllables. I tried to make some small talk but she was not attentive and seemed as if she did not want to talk to me. She fixed her gaze on the telephone on her bedside table, lifted the receiver once and put it down. I also looked in that direction and saw a notebook on which the *"gayatri mantra"* was written in long hand. I asked her if we could defer the clinical examination to some other day to which she readily agreed. She was visibly uncomfortable with my presence. I stood up to take leave of her. She did not stop me, rather she seemed inclined to let me leave; in fact, she showed me the door as if I did not know where I was. I am not sure if I heard her mutter, "Go, in the name of God, go!" I came out and went straight to Nathu Ram who again shrugged his shoulders and gestured with his hands saying, "I don't know anything". I came out thoroughly confused and crestfallen.

I did not know what to do next. I had a full one-and-half hours at hand and I did not want to go back home. Then it occurred to me that I could visit Mr P.N. Dhar, PM's secretary, who lived nearby; lately, I had developed friendly relations with Dhar Sahab and his wife Shiela; Shiela belonged to my community. I am an Agra Mathur and Shiela, a Delhi Mathur. We would often talk and tease each other as to which of these two sub-groups were more talented or cultured. I went to Dhar Saheb's house and rang the bell. Dhar Saheb himself appeared at the door but did not quite open it; I had to push my way in. Dhar Saheb ran back fast and quickly sat on one side of the sofa near the telephone; I followed him and sat on the other side of the sofa. Shiela saw me coming but ignored my presence. Dhar Saheb was also dressed for the day; he too looked tense and confused as if in deep thought, picking up a piece of paper and putting it down.

I tried to make some small talk but he was not interested. We sat silently for several moments. I stood up and asked for leave, moving towards the door. He quickly came after me, opened the door and said the one and the only phrase that morning, *"adab urz"*(greetings) and quietly went back. I came out of their house, thinking *"bahut be-abroo ho kar tere kooche se hum nikle"* (I left your abode under very humiliating circumstances). I went straight to the hospital and got busy with my work, forgetting all about it till Sharada Prasad came to me late in the evening. He was very excited and announced in a loud voice, "You know, India has exploded an atom bomb! This was a top secret event. PM made the announcement in Parliament this afternoon. The explosion occurred at about 8 a.m. PM received the message in code—*'Buddha is smiling'*."

Oh God! that was precisely the time I was with PM, I realized. I understood why I was being shooed away from both houses lest I heard or overheard something before Parliament heard of it which would have been considered a breach of Parliamentary privilege.

The next day, when I met PM she had a mischievous smile which said, "See, how I have fooled you!" Some time after the explosion, it was decided that PM should pay a visit to Pokhran, the site of the explosion. A day was fixed and the programme was drawn up for the visit.

It was a very short visit and again a top secret. PM was to be accompanied by very few people. The security officer and I were included in the retinue; and even I was informed late in the evening, a day before the trip that we were going to Rajasthan. I presumed it would be Jaipur.

I asked her PA but he could not tell me anything as he too did not know anything about the visit. The first leg of our journey to Jodhpur was by plane and from Jodhpur, we flew by helicopter to the explosion site at Pokhran. The earth there had cracked, as far as one could see, with deep long fissures all around. It was a ghastly sight. The chief of the Atomic Energy Commission explained everything to PM and took her around. PM spent about half an hour at the bomb site before it was time to go back.

It seemed during those very days somebody had brought to PM's notice that the fine lattice work in the old Jaisalmer havelis was being vandalized and sold to outside buyers; it was absolutely unacceptable that so much of our fine art should go out of the country in this clandestine manner. PM had, keeping this in mind, indicated that during her next trip to Rajasthan, she would herself pay a visit to Jaislamer to see what could be done.

Having come so close to Jaisalmer, PM decided that she would now go and see for herself the havelis in question and figure out what could be done. This visit was also a top secret and we learnt about it much later. Even the local administration of Jaisalmer had no information about PM's visit. The Collector and SP were on tour; and a junior officer came to receive PM and brought an Ambassador car for her and a couple of jeeps for the others. PM, her security officer and I were accommodated in the car. It was early in the morning and there were very few people on the streets. As we were winding through the streets of Jaisalmer, some people recognized PM in the car and news spread that she was in town. The people were surprised and when we reached the havelis in question and the officer started to explain things and answered her queries a small crowd, consisting mostly of ladies, had collected. A small girl came out of the crowd and questioned PM in a challenging tone, "You are Indira Gandhi?" PM nodded in assent. This was repeated once more and then, the girl, as if she had made a great discovery, exclaimed:

"I have recognized you; you are Indira Gandhi!" PM burst out laughing and, to further satisfy the girl's curiosity, suggested to her, "*Choo kar dekh* (touch and see)." However, someone from behind pulled the girl back and she was lost in the crowd; everyone had a good laugh at PM's sense of humour.

Merely for the sake of
rehabilitating them,
could we put Ranganathan
Maitra, Bhowmik on some
health committee?
Can you suggest some?

NOTE 15 Sanjiv Reddy was the candidate of the Syndicate in 1969 Presidential elections. He lost to Indira Gandhi's candidate, V.V. Giri. The Syndicate later became Congress (O). Indira Gandhi formed Congress (R). Later, Congress (O) came to power in 1977. They made Reddy the President. When Sanjiv Reddy became the President, he had removed Ranganathan, Maitra and Bhowmik from their positions in Red Cross. Indiraji requested that they be reassigned but her request was turned down by Sanjiv Reddy.

OMINOUS EMERGENCY

Sanjay Gandhi had entered politics by the early seventies. PM gradually began to cede ground to him and whatever he did had her tacit approval. She used to say that others only talked but "Sanjay was a doer, a man of action". Sanjay was also the younger son and so, in the hallowed Indian tradition, she pampered him more. PM did not realize that in Sanjay's many actions lay the seeds of her undoing.

After the war with Pakistan and the liberation of Bangladesh, PM was at the height of her popularity, power and glory. She had accumulated so much power in her hands that nobody dare question her or do anything in the government or in the party without consulting her and without her approval. The reservoir of power was overflowing; and power was trickling down and was being often tapped into by Sanjay Gandhi and some members of her personal staff with the help of some pliable officers in the government. But the people outside got the impression that such decisions emanated from PM herself although she had no hand in such decisions. These decisions were unjust and therefore extremely unpopular. Slowly, her popularity was on the decline and resentment against her and more so against Sanjay Gandhi began growing with each passing day.

Public opinion gradually began to turn against Sanjay and his Maruti project, on which he had been working in his factory. There were many allegations including the one that the land had been allotted to him at very low rates by the Congress government in Haryana.This started to create problems for PM because it looked as if everything was being done with her consent.

Sanjay was decent as a person, polite and informal in his behaviour. He was also friendly and helpful. And he was very, very punctual. Every minute counted for him. He was an early riser and he kept away from drinking or smoking. But he was very fond of *lassi*.

He was methodical in everything he did. For example, when he had breakfast, he always took everything in a fixed quantity and this never changed. He would have a certain amount of porridge, put a small potful of cream into that, add a little powdered sugar and stir the entire bowl. He used to keep a medium sized jug of water and drank the whole of it at once. That was the only time he drank water during the day.

Once, a pen of mine got blocked. I knew that Sanjay had a factory with which he was quite hands-on. I asked him if he could unblock the pen for me. The very same day, he did it and brought it back to me. On another occasion, my car conked off. When I reached PM's house, I mentioned this to him. He immediately went out, lifted the bonnet, and fixed it.

In 1974, Sanjay got married to Maneka. She was a friendly person, but she had her own way of doing things, which often did not go down too well with PM. Despite her initial hesitations, PM agreed to the marriage.

Perhaps because of her tender age—Maneka was only 17 at the time, and still a student at Jawaharlal Nehru University—PM and Maneka did not interact much, and had very little in common.

Sonia, who was older when she got married, found the adjustment easier, and settled into the house quickly. She would help the servants with their work, and they certainly had a soft spot for her. Without being overly obsequious, Sonia tried to follow PM's particular way of doing things. Maneka's penchant for riling PM was obvious in the way she tried to bend certain rules. For instance, she would not come down to the dinner table on time, although it was known that PM expected everyone to do so.

Neither staff nor guests were spared from Maneka's frequent jokes. One day after breakfast, she asked me how I liked my eggs. I said I had an omelette, and asked for her preference. With a straight face, she said she swallowed the egg whole, with its shell intact. I realized she was pulling my leg; something she was wont to do.

After Maneka left PM's home, PM and Sonia were very upset, as they doted on Varun who had just been born. He was brought back to the house every evening for some time after Maneka left PM's house. While they were in PM's house, Varun used to sleep in PM's room at night, as she wanted to help the young mother as much as she could.

During those days Mr Raj Narain's petition against PM, in connection with malpractices in her Election campaign in 1972, was being heard in the Allahabad High Court. PM did not realize that the case was going against her till the judgment was delivered on June 12, 1975 and she was unseated. Although initially shocked and surprised, she kept her cool. It seems that her lawyer and her election agent did not pursue the case properly and handle it with the care it deserved. PM herself was summoned to give evidence. Mr Shanti Bhushan, Mr Raj Narain's lawyer, questioned her for about an hour. I could see that she answered every question easily and with a smile. There was a sense of relief over this judgment in the country at large, that a doting mother and her son had been put in their place. Unmindful of all that, she took immediate steps on what had to be done next, legally and politically. On the one hand, an appeal was filed in the Supreme Court immediately against the judgment of the High Court and on the other, the Congress Party organized rallies in Delhi and other parts of the country expressing solidarity with PM, their supreme leader. The Supreme Court, in its wisdom, ordered stay of the judgment, and ruled that a final judgment would be delivered in due course, by a larger bench of the court. All this provided fillip to Mr Jayaprakash Narayan's call for "total revolution".

The movement had already started and was in full swing. JP even called upon the security forces to join the movement even before the Supreme Court could pronounce its final judgment. All this culminated in the Emergency being declared at midnight on June 25th, 1975. This was a clever and tactical move by PM but it also added to the people's frustration and anger.

The main persons behind the imposition of the Emergency were Siddhartha Shankar Ray, Bansi Lal and Sanjay Gandhi. R.K. Dhawan's role in this was limited to following orders. Bansi Lal also had an important role to play in the entire exercise.

Ray was a decent man, but a little arrogant. He was a very clever barrister and a dapper man and rather conscious of the fact. He was on very good terms with PM.

However, it is hard to say how much Ray influenced PM in the decision to impose the Emergency. PM was quite worried herself and genuinely felt that JP's call to the armed forces and police to rise up against her government was a sure-shot recipe for chaos.

It appeared he was attempting a civilian coup and that would have led to a complete breakdown of law and order. In any case, general elections were due in six months and the Opposition could have waited for that before launching its all-out offensive.

In the morning, everybody was stunned to know that Emergency has been clamped the previous night. There was a sense of fear and surprise. Jayaprakash Narayan, Morarji Desai, Charan Singh, Chandra Shekhar and many other opposition leaders had been arrested and jailed. The arrest of JP was particularly distressing, though not many tears might have been shed for Morarji Desai who, though a man of many qualities and unimpeachable integrity, was also egoistic and arrogant with some quaint habits that were laughable. He would propagate his ideas and medicines for health, for any disease or as panacea for health or any ailment. Once Sharada Prasad quizzed me, "Why is Morarji a saint and not a sant"? Finding me at a loss he answered himself, 'Because saint has an 'I,' pointing to Morarji Desai's egocentric personality. But people generally were incensed with JP's arrest and his subsequent incarceration. JP was the prime mover of the protest against PM and Sanjay. In the course of time, he came to acquire a large following of diverse sections of people, big and small, including some Congressmen, thus earning for himself the sobriquet of Lok Nayak.

Another instance related to the rigours of Emergency was the arrest and subsequent incarceration of two Maharanis, Vijayaraje Scindia of Gwalior and Gayatri Devi of Jaipur. Because of our long-standing feudal mentality, an insult to royalty was felt to be particularly galling and continued to be talked about in higher circles of society. Both of them had joined the Swatantra Party which was absolutely antagonistic to Indiraji. Gayatri Devi had come to be ranked as a world class beauty. They were not treated as political detainees but were locked up with common thieves in Tihar Jail. For PM's adversaries like Tarkeshwari Sinha, jealousy was the cause of arrest of these two ladies, as also of the maltreatment and humiliation meted out to them.

Another person who was particularly distressed by the goings on during the Emergency—often attributed to Sanjay Gandhi—and worried about their adverse consequences on PM's politics and her future was Mr B.K. Nehru, who would often come and speak to her about what was happening and the public reaction to these rumours that her younger son was involved. Mr Nehru was then head of the Nehru clan and PM had great respect for him and particularly for his wife Fori, who was both her aunt and a friend. On one occasion, Mr Nehru perhaps, told PM a lot more than was necessary and might have used some strong words, which apparently created friction and disharmony. When I went to see her the next morning I found her sitting on her office table, depressed and angry as I had never seen before. She asked me if I knew Mr Biju Nehru at all, meaning B.K. Nehru. I replied that I had met Mr Nehru a couple of times in her house and not much more. She briefly narrated to me the previous day's incident.

"Mr Nehru is head of the family", she said and she had great respect for him and he had, perhaps, reprimanded her during their discussions. She was virtually in tears and could not speak any further. Seeing her so depressed and downcast, I tried to enliven her mood by reciting an Urdu couplet *"ajab sulagti huyi lakriya hain yah kambakht rishteydar / agar pass rahe to jala kare. Door rahe toh dhua de.* (Strange tinders are these relatives. They burn with envy when close and billow smoke from afar)." She laughed at it. Since she was ready she left immediately for her office. In the office, a little later in the day, she narrated this incident, including the Urdu couplet, to her secretary, Mr P.N. Dhar, who phoned me immediately. Mr Dhar was quite amused and expressed his appreciation for my "poetic genius".

Except for the first few days after the declaration of emergency, when she spent a good bit of her time at home with her advisers, PM's and Sanjay Gandhi's authoritarianism kept on increasing. Press censorship was clamped, and no one could raise a voice of dissent. There was fear all round and nobody felt secure. Fear of "the unknown" was all pervading. But fear so generated also led to some discipline and a sense of purpose and positive gains. Things were moving. Trains were running on time, and sanitation and policing improved and so also the PDS and other similar services. But in a couple of months, things started to go wrong.

To stress the supreme authority of PM, sycophants had coined a slogan "Indira is India and India is Indira". Thousands of people were put in jail all across the country. The discontent against PM and Sanjay was growing by the hour and she was fast losing her people's confidence and sympathy. Elections too had been postponed causing further alienation. PM herself was not satisfied with the state of affairs, but somehow she did not intervene and let it go on. Perhaps she had become a victim of the tyranny of the excessive love she had for her younger son. PM herself was feeling the pinch but even then when some friends like Subhadra Joshi and K.C. Pant and relatives like B.K. Nehru wanted to tell Sanjay some home truths, PM dissuaded them from speaking to him lest he be rude to them.

At the same time, Sanjay also announced his own five-point programme in addition to PM's 20-point programme. The programme of family planning was started at the behest of Sanjay Gandhi under which forced sterilizations were conducted on persons not quite willing. Targets, i.e., number of operations were fixed for officials, affecting their chances of promotion and they were punished if they failed to meet the targets. Vasectomy certificates were demanded for a variety of facilities normally provided by the government to every citizen of the country. This sometimes produced ridiculous situations. For example, one morning, a retired elderly Army Colonel approached PM during her daily meeting with the public, "*darshan*" as it came to be known, and complained that when he went to the DDA for registration of a flat, he was asked to produce his vasectomy certificate before he could be registered.

Since I happened to be there at that moment she sent for me and expressed her anger and disgust. Raising her voice, she questioned me, "who is doing all that?"although she knew very well that I was not concerned with the matter. I came away and found that a prominent lady worker actively involved in the family planning operations, happened to be there, and I told her about PM's objections to her FP Operations. She tried to give some excuse and explanation while promising to see what could be done.

In the name of beautification and slum clearance, demolition of buildings and sometimes old standing houses was undertaken. Demolition in the Turkman Gate area acquired special notoriety.

Muslims were already alienated by the sterilization drive and Turkman Gate area housed a large number of Muslims. So the situation worsened there in no time.

Rukhsana Sultana, a friend of Sanjay's, was also involved in the sterilization operations, organizing camps and persuading people to come to these. She could at best be described as a socialite, as she had no experience whatsoever in politics.

Navin Chawla, private secretary to the Delhi Lieutenant Governor, Kishen Chand, at that time, got along very well with Sanjay and his role was to ensure that whatever Sanjay desired was carried out by the Delhi Administration.

The people's resentment against PM and Sanjay Gandhi had reached new depths and PM also felt that such a situation should not be allowed to continue any longer. JP's call to the Army and the police to disobey orders that they thought were unjust was particularly alarming: a sure invitation to anarchy and chaos. "Enough is enough", she thought. Similar advice was given to her by some of her trusted bureaucrats, Even her own partymen were unhappy and restive, and believed that elections should be held forthwith. The continued denial of civil rights would also dent her image in foreign countries.

PM also felt convinced that the same should be done. She withdrew the Emergency on March 21, 1977 just as suddenly as she had imposed it and announced General Elections.

There were certain ominous signs before the elections were announced by PM. P.N. Dhar, who had strongly advised PM to hold elections, suffered the loss of his mother-in-law—to whom he was very close—on the day the General Elections were announced. The President, Fakhruddin Ali Ahmed, also passed away during those very days.

The surprise move on her part caused great relief and excitement across the country. Political parties started preparing themselves for elections and also, if possible, to come together to defeat the Congress. Under the leadership of Jayaprakash Narayan, called the "Lok Nayak", a conglomerate of disparate political parties was formed, called the Janata Party.

There was nothing in common between them which would hold them together except a common desire to defeat the Congress and remove Indira Gandhi and her son from power. The glitter of power and self-interest attracted them to each other, in which also lay the fulfillment of their long-cherished desire and dream.

The Emergency having been lifted and political normalcy restored, political parties began organizing rallies and the JP's revolution had also gathered momentum. PM could see the gathering storm, but she did not lose her cool.

Whatever the result, she would do her duty towards the country and win the election if possible and avert the disaster waiting to happen if the police and Army were to revolt in response to JP's call. She started her election tours and organized public meetings. These meetings were thinly attended, but PM continued to make forceful speeches outlining her policy and programmes. As luck would have it, during those very days she developed severe "Herpes Zoster" on the face, a particularly painful condition, and even her eyes were under threat.

Despite being quite unwell, she did not stop but continued with her activities of touring and campaigning. I was with her all the time praying for her health and my reputation.

Sanjay was not aggressive in personal life although he could be rude sometimes. He had a short fuse where discussions and arguments were concerned. If you did not agree with him, his face would turn red and he would get up and walk out. He did not like to be contradicted. Never abusive, anyone he did not like was called "*nikamma*" (a nincompoop).

Sycophants continued to meet PM here and there during her election tours, giving inflated estimates of attendance at the public meetings. And she would accept such information with a touch of disdain.

After the voting was over and the results were announced, the Janata Party under JP scored a resounding victory. The Congress was routed in the entire North India, but in Southern states their showing was not bad. Both Sanjay and PM lost the elections. There was jubilation across the country that the authoritarian family regime has been eliminated and a new democratic era would dawn. PM accepted her defeat gracefully with her usual cool and composure. When some people tried to show sympathy with her, she kept smiling and merely shrugged her shoulders saying "it just happens, so what". Sanjay also accepted the defeat nonchalantly.

Having lost the elections because of her own acts of commission and omission coupled with the disloyalty of old friends and her own partymen who left her like mice running from a sinking ship PM had no other option except to resign. She handed over her letter of resignation to Mr B.D. Jatti, who was the acting President after the untimely demise of Fakhruddin Saheb at his residence.

The very evening she demitted office, she held a garden party at her official residence where all secretaries to the government and other members of the staff working for her in the office and at the house were invited. We all assembled and stood in a semi-circle. Going round the circle, PM thanked everyone individually with folded hands. Sometimes she had a word of advice for someone and a witty remark for another; she was always in smiles as if nothing had happened. I was standing at the end of the curve when she came up to me. She had some belated advice to give, "If you had utilized your time well, instead of following me all the time and everywhere, you could have become the best-read man in the country."

I quietly accepted the advice, as this was no time to match wits. I could have said "It was my duty to do so", but did not. Anything else would have amounted to dereliction of duty. After meeting everybody she left the party with her usual composure, a glint in her eyes and a smile on her face. Reaching the gate she raised her right hand and looked back just once as if to say, "Cheerio folks, but this is not the end of the road."

The very next day she applied herself to finding a house where she would now have to live—the present house went with the office. She was neither an MP nor a minister nor a government servant entitled to any kind of government accommodation. The old family friend, Mohammad Yunus, vacated his own house for her and even lent the services of his cook to start the kitchen. It was a small house with only four rooms and the family moved with her and adjusted themselves in this house. One room for PM, one for Rajiv and family and the third for Sanjay and Maneka, leaving a small side room for visitors who would drop in sometimes. Among the servants only Nathu Ram, her old valet, came with her. She had no PA or private secretary—government servants having been withdrawn and sent to their respective positions.

I continued to see her every morning, as was my practice since a decade earlier, ever since she took me as her doctor in June, 1966.

After shifting to the new house, PM took a few days to collect her thoughts and decide her future course of action. This she had to do all by herself; there was no friend or colleague whose advice she could seek even for an informal chat or discussion. In fact, she was feeling lonely as if abandoned by everyone except the immediate family. Sanjay was now her sole advisor and confidant. Dhawan was there for consultation and advice but he also had to devote his time to defend himself in court, Indiraji and Sanjay and to attend to the enquires which had already been set in motion. One or two ladies—Bibi Amtus Salam, Saroj Kapade, Kumudben Joshi—and some other co-workers in the Congress Party would make an appearance now then. PM woke up at the usual time, took her breakfast, went through four or five newspapers of the day, but with nothing positive to do and no visitors to meet. To keep herself busy she would pace between the few rooms of the house—and there weren't too many rooms either. Always a perfectionist, she would adjust the furniture, pictures and wall hangings, rearrange the carpets etc. and dust her own room or peep into the kitchen to keep herself busy. She had no office, no staff car or even a car of her own. The staff car allotted to her had already been withdrawn and she had no telephone operator to help her and she had forgotten the telephone numbers of friends. Her adversaries even spread rumours that she had lost her mental balance and that she moved around the house aimlessly with her eyes and mouth wide open. Some well wishers advised her that she should detach herself from Sanjay and ask him to stay elsewhere because in their eyes it was Sanjay whose misadventures and abrasive behaviour and mannerisms had antagonized everyone resulting in her own fall as well as that of the party. One morning she casually mentioned this to me: "Don't you think that in such times of adversity we should stay together and not appear to be a house divided." This she said with an air of finality and satisfaction.

In the meantime, the Central Government headed by the Janata Party dismissed the Congress governments in all states except Kerala on the pretext that the Congress had lost the confidence of the people and in their place Janata Party governments were installed.

One morning when I went to see her during my daily visits she mentioned to me that Bhagwat Dayal Sharma, the then Chief Minister of Haryana, was taken ill and admitted to AIIMS and has expressed his desire to meet PM and if PM would be kind enough to meet him in the hospital. She did not have a car to take her to the hospital as a friend used to send his car every morning for her use. Since she was not sure of the car being there that morning, she came out to see for herself whether any other vehicle was available for her going to AIIMS to meet Sharmaji. There was no other car except mine parked on the side and she enquired as to whose car it was.

When I told her it was mine, her immediate response was, "Why not take this car, what is wrong with it?" I gestured to her why not, and brought the car out. My car was a small Fiat and I opened the door of the back seat and she got in. I got into the driver's seat. A little surprised, she asked me,

"Why! You do not have a driver?"

"No, I drive myself" I replied.

"I can't treat you as a driver".

She got out and came up to the door of the bucket seat. I opened the door and she sat there. I drove her down to the AIIMS where she met Sharmaji and stayed with him for about 20 minutes. Just as we were coming out, someone came towards us and informed that the Urdu poet Firaq Gorakhpuri was also admitted on the same floor and had requested PM to meet him. She immediately agreed and we went to see Firaq Sahib. PM spent a few minutes with him and talked about some old friends from Allahabad days. I drove her back home. There was no fuss, no security, and wonder of wonders, a former Prime Minister and perhaps also a future Prime Minister driving down with a mere government doctor on the front seat of a small Fiat car without any security. Such things do happen sometimes!

The president is
dead set against
anyone who was in the
Red Cross previously &
refuses to put in
[illegible] a
[illegible]. I did not
mention Bhowmick.
What about Begum
Ali Yavar Jung as
Chairman & some
new people?

NOTE 16 After the President's refusal to re-appoint Sanjiv Reddy, PM send this note. "The President is dead set against anyone who was in the Red Cross previously", and that he was making alternative arrangements by appointing Begum Ali Yavar Jung as Chairman.

THE JANTA FLIP FLOP

The Janta Party was victorious in the elections held in 1977. But from the very beginning it was apparent that they were going to fall apart soon. Mutual recrimination, suspicions of each other's motives, and past experience had already made them adversaries of each other and, therefore, unable to run a government smoothly for any common or laudable objective, without which no coalition can be functional or even survive.

As the majority party defeated the Congress comprehensively, the President called the president of Janata Party, i.e., Jayaprakash Narayan, to form the government. The cracks within the Janta Party had started showing already and things were not moving at all. By hard means and the sheer force of his personality, JP and the Janata Party were able to form a government with Morarji Desai as Prime Minister and other members of the party taking up other portfolios but not in any spirit of mutual trust or a desire to work as a cohesive team. Even during the swearing-in ceremony, a couple of ministers absented themselves, though after a few days they consented to join the Cabinet but only after a lot of protests and subsequent persuasion. I remember that George Fernandes and Raj Narain were two such ministers. News about their dissent and snarling at each other was getting into the public glare and the media. Even Cabinet meetings had lost their decorum and strong words were sometimes used against each other. All this was in the air and sometimes even reported in the press. The public was disillusioned and unfavourable comparisons between Janata Party's and Indira Gandhi's times began to be made. No decisions were being taken by the government and nothing appeared to be moving. Sympathy for Indira Gandhi, though not yet for Sanjay Gandhi, was becoming evident, as also the widening fissures within the Janata Government.

Sometime during the month of July 1977, a most unfortunate incident happened in a remote village in Bihar called Belchi where upper caste land-owners massacred a number of Harijans over some land dispute. For lack of communication, this information took a couple of days to reach Delhi. However, the Janta government failed to take any action. Indira Gandhi always had sympathy for Dalits and other deprived sections. She immediately decided to visit Belchi with some fellow congressmen. It was rainy season and this remote village was marooned making it very difficult to reach but she was determined, travelling by jeep and tractors. Ultimately with her courage and determination she reached Belchi in the dark of night riding on an elephant. She was thoroughly moved when the villagers related to her their tales of woe and how little had been done by the government to help them. All this she narrated to me on her return. I could imagine from her tone and temper the pain the she was carrying for the fate that had fallen upon these poor and miserable villagers of Belchi.

The Janta government was cracking and breaking into constituent parties and others who for their own sake had brought it into being. No one seemed to have a long term and consolidated view and a plan for the betterment of the country or even their own by proper planning to ensure long term benefits.

And for some, especially Charan Singh, the only programme appeared to be to punish Indiraji and Sanjay. Commissions of enquiry were set up to go into excesses of emergency and especially Sanjay's programme of demolition and family planning.

One of these enquiry commissions, notably Shah Commission, headed by a former Chief Justice, J.C. Shah, generated a lot of interest, almost like a popular film or a theatre performance. These commissions were created in haste without going into details of law, their mandate, powers, procedure, etc. The hearings were held in Patiala House where loud speakers were installed outside the court room for the benefit of hundreds of people who wanted to hear the proceedings.

But in reality, it was for those who wanted to see Indira and Sanjay Gandhi arrested, humiliated and shouted at. In course of time these proceedings lost their seriousness. People were coming and going and walking freely inside the court room, making their own submissions for which they themselves were not prepared but more often than not these were just emotional outbursts at a certain point of time. They had really come only to hear and enjoy the fun of the proceedings of the court. Sanjay appeared before the commission a number of times with his wife Maneka who often joked with Justice Shah and other functionaries which became a source of entertainment for the assembled people. Justice Shah himself did not appear to know how to go about his business, obviously because the terms of reference of the commission were vague and unclear. Indira Gandhi appeared once or twice but she and her lawyer were able to foil all efforts by the Commission to catch her.

Initially, PM felt a bit lonely after losing the elections. She had nothing to do. No files would come to her. Newspapers were all she had to read. Even her friends had deserted her. Only her family was there. I used to go every morning as before. In the morning, she would get ready like before but there would be nowhere to go.

There were rumours that she had lost her mind because she would go around all the rooms adjusting the furniture and the curtains, etc. But she was a perfectionist and she used to do this even on tours, at least in her own room.

Incidentally, in those very days, a Hollywood film titled "Jaws, Paws and Claws" was showing at a local cinema hall. The title amused me a little and I mentioned this to my friend Sharada Prasad, who was equally surprised and amused. "Is it a movie?" he asked. "Yes, it is", I said, "actors—all animals, no humans in it".

Sharada laughed and said, "oh! I thought this was a documentary of the cabinet meeting of the Janta Party". We had a good laugh over his wisecrack. After a few days when I narrated this incident to Indiraji, she also had a good laugh but ruefully remarked, "if that is so, what will they achieve for the good of the country?"

I was told by a friend who was in the know of things, and also close to some people in the Janta Party, that my visits to Indiraji were not being liked by the Health Minister, Raj Narain. I made it clear to my friend that it was a matter of medical ethics as well as loyalty, and I continued to do my duty towards her as always.

Sanjay continued to be busy with his Maruti project, leaving home for his factory early morning every day.

What was going on inside the Janta government was now in the public domain. As the Janata Party started disintegrating, Congressmen started to come back to Indiraji.

It was clear that the Janta government was going to break into pieces, till one day Morarji Desai, finally, disgusted and unable to hold his government to any purposeful existence, submitted his resignation to the President on July 13, 1979. The President dissolved the Parliament and ordered General Elections on August 22, 1979 and asked Charan Singh to form a caretaker Government.

One morning as I was coming out of Indiraji's house, a former MP saw me and taunted me, "Doctor, to see you come back means that happy days are coming soon". I rejoined, "you fool, I was always here; to see you come back means that those good days are coming back". Laughing together, we both jumped into a happy embrace, amongst ourselves assured of the future. By that time Congressmen had also realized that their best interest lay in coming back to Indiraji again and working jointly hand in hand for the victory of the Congress party under her leadership. Indiraji made a whirlwind tour of the country, covering 40,000 miles, addressing about 20 meetings per day. People were awake again. The Congress party and Indiraji won the election hands down—351 of the total 542 seats in Lok Sabha. Indiraji won the elections from both seats she had contested, Rae Bareilly in UP and Medak in Andhra Pradesh. Sanjay too had a comfortable victory from Amethi in UP Janta Party was completely decimated and except for a few of their top leaders, all others lost the elections and vanished into thin air; never to be seen again. JP's revolution had devoured its own children.

Indiraji now had a very comfortable majority in the Lok Sabha and there was virtually no opposition left to stand in her way. After this decisive victory the President invited Indiraji to form the government. Hurried and hectic consultations were held between Indiraji and some of her colleagues who had won the elections, with Sanjay again being the main advisor. Names of Cabinet Ministers were being drawn up. Morarji had already vacated the house and some repairs, etc. were being done and readied for Indiraji to move in.

One morning when I went to see her on my usual rounds, I found her sitting on her bed reading an open newspaper and another newspaper opened wide and spread on the bed. As I entered her room, she asked, "look, have you seen this?

Since I had not, I went up and looked at the paper and picked it up. What I found was a cartoon captioned with a limerick:

"There was a young lady of Riga/ Who rode with a smile on a tiger/ They returned from the ride/ With the lady inside/ And a smile on the face of the tiger."

The cartoon showed a tiger badly mauled and lying dead, skin ripped and torn, rib cage showing, tail turned into a rope, mouth wide open, all teeth broken, blood oozing out, one limb lying broken and a girl standing beside it, smiling wide and clear.

In this fresh flush of glory and success she must have felt extremely happy to see this cartoon. It was a humorous but sad commentary on the recent political events in the country.

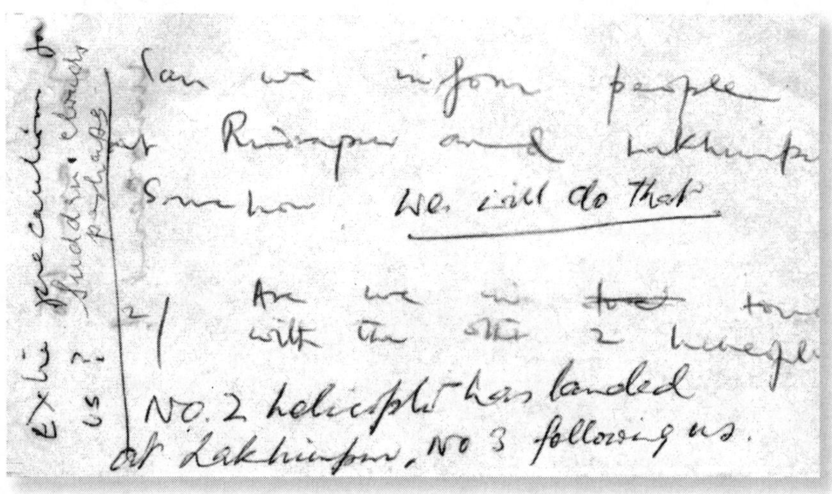

Can we inform people at Rampur and Lakhimpur

Somehow We will do that

2/ Are we in touch with the other 2 helicopters

No. 2 helicopter has landed at Lakhimpur, No 3 following us.

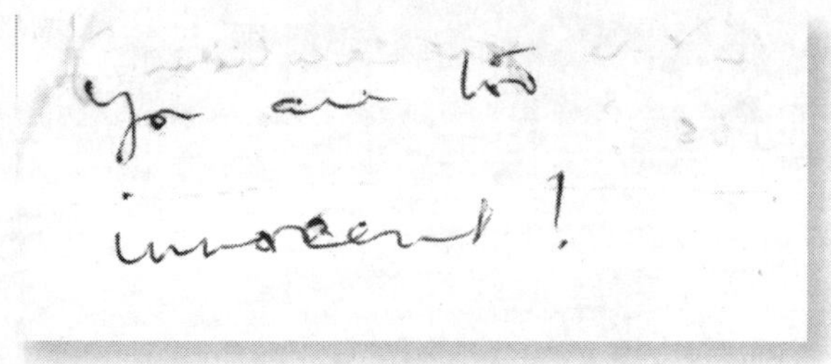

You are too innocent!

NOTE 17 Usually as a security measure, PM's helicopter was followed by two others. On one occasion, on our way to Lakhimpur, the helicopter after ours landed first. On finding out about it, PM sent me a note about it. In my reply, I reasoned that maybe it was an extra security measure or because of the weather. She replied with a "you are too innocent!" We were to, later, find out that it was because the pilot in the helicopter behind ours was related to an officer in Lakhimpur.

AT VINOBA'S SIDE

It was learnt in the latter half of 1982 that Vinoba Bhave or "Baba", as the inmates of his Ashram and others affectionately and respectfully called him, had caught a severe chest infection. He was critically ill, not responding to antibiotic therapy and had been put on continuous oxygen. Doctors had little hope. PM had immense respect for him, despite some very unsavoury remarks that Baba had made against her during Emergency, and wanted to go and see him at his Ashram in Paunar, near Nagpur. It was so arranged that she would go by air to Nagpur and then drive down to Paunar, about 30 km from there.

Her plan was to spend the day at the Ashram, leave in the evening and reach Nagpur and spend the night at the Raj Bhawan and take a flight to Delhi in the morning. We reached Paunar in the afternoon. PM first went straight to meet and pay her respects to "Baba". Thereafter, we had lunch. It was an Ashram-style lunch. We all sat on mats on the floor and the food was served in typical *"desi"* style, in *thalis, katoras,* etc. It was a frugal Ashram meal consisting of dal (almost like pea soup) with a few grains that could survive the boiling, rice, roti smeared with ghee, achar, chutney and curd. I had a detailed discussion with the doctors attending on Vinobaji who were doing their best.

His condition was poor, according to them. PM continued to sit with Vinobaji, coming out occasionally to meet Congressmen who would gather in groups to have a word with her. Time was running out and we were getting close to our schedule for departure. PM sent for me and questioned about the Baba's condition, in order to decide whether to go back as per the programme or stay in the Ashram for the night. She asked me to talk to the doctors before deciding whether to leave or not. Sensing all this uncertainty, somebody claimed that the police, for security reasons, were not in favour of PM staying at the Ashram for the night. When PM learnt of this, she was a little upset.

"These fellows don't understand the delicacy of the situation," she said and instructed me to have a word with the security people. The DIG in-charge of security told me emphatically that it was not for security reasons; according to him, they were duty-bound to provide security wherever she decided to stay, but it was for reasons of her personal comfort that some people were concerned. After all, he said, it was an Ashram. PM finally decided that she would spend the night at the Ashram. Having come all the way, she did not wish to do anything that might have looked like running away in haste.

Having taken the decision, PM asked me to see what could be done for her stay in the Ashram at night. The keeper of the Ashram showed me the only room available and was quite apologetic because even that room was untidy. It appeared that a *pahalwan* had been staying there and getting his "*tel malish*" (massage) every day—oil was smeared all over the place.

There was a solitary hospital bed with the mattress almost soaked in oil, although there was an attached bathroom and toilet with a plastic bucket, and a mug with a broken handle. The keeper was very apologetic, but assured us that he would get the floor and bathroom cleaned up at once.

I asked him if the mattress could be changed but there were none available in the Ashram. He advised me to visit the local Khadi Bhandar and get whatever was necessary; he added that only Khadi Bhandar stuff was used in the Ashram. Accordingly, I brought a new mattress, a couple of bed-sheets and towels, a plastic bucket, two mugs and a cake of soap, namely "Neem", the only one available in the Khadi Bhandar. We had dinner in the Ashram after which she went to take leave of Baba for the night. I escorted and brought PM to her room. Her immediate reaction upon entering the room was, "this is all right; why not." She spent the night in those very austere surroundings and was absolutely satisfied, she had no complaints.

PM could feel equally comfortable not only in some Maharaja's palace, or in four or five-star hotels but also in a sadhu's ashram, like the one at Paunar.

Vinobaji passed away a few days later, much mourned by Indiraji and the rest of the nation.

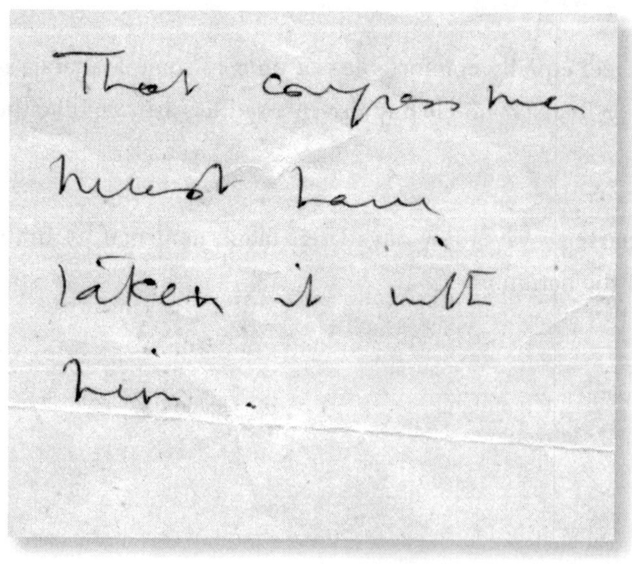

That congressman
must have
taken it with
him.

NOTE 18 When something had gone missing at home, PM sent me a note saying "that Congressman must have taken it with him."

RELATIONS WITH FOREIGN DIGNITARIES

PM's relations with foreign heads of government and other foreign dignitaries were cordial, and based on equality, mutual respect, trust and enlightened national interest, broad guidelines for which had already been laid down by an august forebear of hers, Emperor Porus of Taxila.

Though vanquished in war by Alexander, when asked by the great Greek general, "How should I treat you", prompt came the reply from Porus, "Just as one king treats another."

With some leaders her relations were particularly good, who held her in special esteem, some of whose greatness would rub onto lesser people like me.

In the earlier years of her premiership, I went with her on a state visit to Cairo. We were guests of the Egyptian President Gamal Abdel Nasser and were lodged in the Cubbeh Palace, the palace vacated by King Farouk of Egypt who was dethroned after a military coup led by the former. President Nasser also held his office in the same building. One afternoon, there was a programme for PM to visit some institution and

President Nasser was to accompany her. Since some of us on duty always accompanied her on such engagements, I also got ready, and was standing in the verandah with others, when we saw the President coming out and towards where we were standing. We greeted him respectfully bowing down and did "Namaskar". He responded with a half military salute, then came up and shook hands with each one of us; perhaps that was because we were Indira Gandhi's men—a most gracious gesture on the part of the President.

A couple of times PM was invited by President Tito of Yugoslavia to pay a State visit. On one occasion the President received us at his sea resort on an island, Brioni. We were lodged in a hotel but PM stayed in a villa next to the President's. The next day, President Tito drove PM around the island in his white Mercedes which he used to drive himself. In the afternoon, he took us all for a cruise around a number of islands near Brioni. We were taken around in the President's own yacht, with exquisite food and all kinds of drinks all the way. A person was giving a running commentary in English describing the beautiful islands in front of our eyes. At one point he wanted to be a little funny and loudly announced, "ladies and gentlemen, the island in front of your eyes is called the Nudists' Paradise". Everyone unabashedly strained their necks forward to see if they could witness something interesting. At that he laughed loudly and everyone else, including President Tito, also laughed with him, but we felt so embarrassed for having been fooled.

The atmosphere was one of informality and cordiality. Such great bonhomie was shown to PM and her party in some countries.

The special relationship between PM, President Nasser and President Tito was presumably an extension of the Non-aligned Movement in which these two leaders were Panditji's colleagues and trustworthy friends.

Once, as state guests on a visit to the beautiful Pacific island of Tonga, the King and Queen invited PM and party for lunch and a cultural show which was held in the open on a large enough lawn.

PM and senior members of our delegation and some Tongan dignitaries sat at a high table with the King and Queen, but we were divided into several groups, seated on bamboo mats on the ground under a tent. Typical Tongan food was already served; and also a lovely Tongan girl was attached to each group waiting to help. Senior members of the delegation were introduced to the King and Queen. When Dr P.C. Alexander was introduced, the Queen thought that he was the medical doctor and exclaimed, "Oh, you are the doctor." Alexander made a hasty retreat saying, "No, no, not me, there is another man." I was sent for and Dr Alexander introduced me to the King and Queen and I respectfully bowed to both. The Queen was gracious enough to shake hands, but the King merely smiled. The Queen gestured to me to sit on a nearby chair and also pointed towards the table still with a lot of sea food and fruits as if to say, "go ahead and help yourself." I felt honoured.

Likewise, the President of Austria treated PM with great affection and regard, much more than the requirements of protocol. The Ambassador later explained to me the cause of this extra show of affection. He said that PM had met the President on one of Panditji's earlier visits to Austria when she had accompanied her father. Later, Panditji and the Austrian President had become good friends and it was the President's wish that Panditji's daughter should visit Austria now that she herself was the Prime Minister of India.

While we were in Austria, PM underwent an eye check-up. For some time, she had been complaining about some problem with her eyes. Our doctors did not see anything much in it. However, PM wanted to make sure there was no problem and wished for a second opinion. On the advice of some well-meaning friends in India and her own good impression about Austrian doctors who had earlier treated her mother, PM underwent a check-up by an Austrian doctor, who found that she was in perfect health and had also said a few words complimenting me for the good care I had taken of her. This information was apparently conveyed to the President. In the evening, the President held a reception in honour of PM to which all of us were also invited. He complimented PM for her good health and also expressed a desire to see her doctor. I was summoned. The President shook hands with me and said something with a smile which I could not follow. As a prize, I received a medical bag as a special gift from the President of Austria.

Again in Czechoslovakia, it so happened that Shubhash Tandon's (our Chief of Security) birthday fell on a day during PM's visit to that country. The Czech Prime Minister had got to know about this, perhaps, from some member of his own security staff who had gotten friendly with us. When he came to meet PM, Tandon and other members of the delegation were waiting outside PM's room. The protocol officer there introduced us individually to the Czech Prime Minister, who greeted Tandon with a "Happy Birthday, Mr Tandon".

Later, when Tandon went to his room, he found a birthday cake from the Czech PM waiting. During PM's visit to the USA in July 1982, at the White House banquet in Washington, when it was over and it was time for everyone to leave, President Reagan and the lady came out into the portico with PM to see her off to her car. Since Dhawan and I were in PM's convoy, we also came out behind her and were standing nearby in a corner waiting for our car. The lady Protocol Officer with a very distinguished name (Mrs Roosevelt) came and introduced us to the President, who was gracious enough to shake hands with us individually.

The lady just stood with a pleasing smile. A photographer, who was standing nearby, clicked a photo, a copy of which was sent to me and that was with me till the other day when my brother, who lives in the US, discovered it and pinched it away, saying, "No use of this lying with you, I will show it off to my friends in the US and tell them, that this is my brother in the White House". No Joke! Again, all this because we were Indira Gandhi's men.

But it was not always so pleasant and cordial; sometimes there were discordant notes. A Western leader who was bent upon displaying his "the arrogance of power" while meeting PM, forgot to show even the most elementary courtesy between human beings, to say nothing of observing diplomatic etiquette. But fate had decreed that the same leader would also prove the veracity of the old maxim, "pride goeth before a fall".

On the contrary, President Fiedel Castro of Cuba, not content with just shaking hands with PM, unabashedly hugged her, calling her his sister, from the podium of the Non-Alignment Summit in Delhi in March 1983, in full view of TV cameras and the world press, and publicly demonstrated his affection and regard for our Prime Minister.

Once when President Zia of Pakistan complained to PM about getting bad press, PM consoled him and advised, "Don't worry about these pressmen, they know nothing; Look, they call you a democrat and me a dictator!" The President was not amused!

The most notable foreign dignitary to visit India during these years—it may even be unfair to call him a foreigner was Badshah Khan, respectfully called the Frontier Gandhi for his sacrifices and the part he played in the freedom struggle following the path of non-violence showed by Gandhiji. This great Pathan leader went to jail a number of times in British India, but he was incarcerated for a much longer period in Pakistan. When the North Western Frontier Provinces (NWFP), his home state, became a part of Pakistan after partition, technically he became a Pakistani citizen but did not quite accept Pakistani citizenship and made no secret of it, and continued to regard himself as an Indian.

He came to India after 22 years for Mahatma Gandhi's birth centenary on October 2, 1969. He had already spent 27 years in Pakistani jails. PM and many other leaders who had worked with him during the freedom movement were at the airport to receive him. I also went to the airport and could see the grand old man looking quite fit with a glow on his face, in disheveled *khadi* clothes, a stick in one hand and a bundle of all his possessions in the other. He was given a tumultuous welcome wherever he went. He spent a few days in the country and went to a few other cities also.

During his second visit to India in 1981, the grand old man was not in the best of health. He was given a check-up and treatment at the hands of some Bombay doctors. I accompanied him on his way back to Peshawar. On the way, I had occasion to exchange a few words with him, a truly great man of our age. I also spent a few hours with his family in Peshawar.

His son, Wali Khan, and his family had also not quite accepted the fact of the partition of India and never saw themselves as citizens of Pakistan; they were always critical of Pakistan and its policies towards India and therefore, had to pay for their views by spending a long time in jail.

A watch gifted by Rajiv Gandhi which I still wear

TWO CHARMING LADIES

Undoubtedly, Margaret Thatcher was a firm, decisive and determined politician who did so much for her country. A grateful nation respectfully nicknamed her the "Iron Lady" and that is how she came to be known the world over. But by the time Mrs Thatcher came on the world stage, PM had been there for more than a decade and had already made a mark for herself as a world leader, one who had to be counted.

Respecting her age and seniority, Mrs Thatcher showed due deference towards PM.

Much later, I happened to see a photograph of the Iron Lady sitting in her car, leaving her official 10, Downing Street residence, after demitting office as Prime Minister; she seemed weighed down by deceit and defeat, and her eyes and face were red, with tears rolling down her cheek. She probably was thinking, "what an end; and it will never be the same again!"

PM was also a very firm, decisive, courageous and determined administrator with a strong will power. She was also elegant and petite at the same time. I remember, an instance when shopping in a bookstore in Paris, the people on the streets and around got to know that she was inside the bookstore. A sizeable crowd collected at the door of the shop to have a good look at her. As PM came out to get into her car, the crowd burst into loud cheers and clapping. A lady in the crowd could not control herself and looking at PM, exclaimed; "*petite, petite!*" and everyone in the crowd joined in the chorus. She could not imagine how so much courage, strength and will power as well as grace was packed in the diminutive frame of this petite lady.

I happened to see these two great leaders together a couple of times. At the Cancun Conference in Mexico on October 22 and 23, 1981, Mrs Thatcher and PM and our delegation were staying in the same hotel—newly constructed but not quite ready for occupation and which had only one lift then.

Mrs Thatcher was put up on the top floor, and we, a few floors down. In the morning when everybody was in a rush to get to the meeting venue on time, the lift while coming down would be full when it reached our floor; there was no way PM and Dr Alexander could get in.

The lift would not even stop. Tandon and I did not like the idea of PM waiting and being left out. The two of us thought of a plan—to take the lift on its journey up as far as it would go, and while coming down make it stop at our floor. The two of us would then step out of the lift and PM and Dr Alexander could step in. Mrs Thatcher, who was there, having got in from her floor, would deferentially greet PM with a "good morning" and then squeeze herself behind her people to make room for PM. Such was the regard the Iron Lady had for PM. The two would then smile and exchange friendly glances.

On another occasion in November 1983, when the Commonwealth Prime Ministers' conference was held in New Delhi and the "retreat" for the leaders was organized in Goa, PM and Mrs Thatcher and others were staying in the same hotel. As was my habit, I got ready quite early in the morning and came down and stood at the lobby door waiting for PM. I thought that if she would like to go somewhere, I could accompany her. I saw PM and Dr Alexander coming towards the door. And from a distance, PM looked at me said and something to Dr Alexander who came up and told me,. "PM has remarked that you are over-dressed. "Why is the doctor over-dressed?" I explained to Dr Alexander, "PM is on holiday but I am on duty, that's why." To meet the requirements of the retreat, he advised, "take off your tie, put it in your pocket, take off your jacket and let it hang on the shoulders and see, now you are also properly dressed!" PM was wearing salwar kameez and canvas PT shoes, Mrs Thatcher was dressed in slacks and blouse, both in their holiday attire and mood. PM and Margaret Thatcher greeted each other quite loudly and were coming towards the door where two of us, Dr Alexander and I were standing. PM, addressing, Dr Alexander said, "We don't seem to have made any arrangement for the ladies for shopping or sight-seeing." Before Dr Alexander could reply, Mrs Thatcher intervened, "Don't worry about the ladies, leave them to Dennis" (her husband who had accompanied her on this visit) "he knows how to handle the ladies." The two leaders had a good laugh and almost ran, like schoolgirls, for a picnic on the beach. Mrs Thatcher apparently enjoyed her funny remark about her husband.

Once in Moscow, at the height of the Russian winter to attend the funeral of one of the Soviet leaders, the two leaders were together again in the same lodging. I was walking down with PM from the Kremlin Palace to the Red Square where the ceremony was being held. The ground was slippery with slush and snow and I could see Margaret Thatcher walking behind her, struggling hard to catch up with PM but her stilettos would not let her walk fast. But PM had no difficulty in walking down since she was in her gumboots. I brought to PM's notice Mrs Thatcher's plight in trying to catch up. "Let her", she whispered in reply but stopped for a while. The two of them then exchanged greetings and Mrs Thatcher, looking at PM's gumboots, said something that I could not catch. PM said a word of praise for her valet for being careful about these things.

Mrs Thatcher responded, "I wish I had one like him too." Such friendly banter and informality, just like any two female friends anywhere else!

प्रधान मंत्री भवन
PRIME MINISTER'S HOUSE
NEW DELHI

January 11, 1974.

Dear Dr. Mathur,

I am deeply grieved to hear of your father's passing away. I can understand what it means to lose a parent and what a void it leaves in one's life. I wish you had remained in Kanpur instead of motoring all the way to Jhansi but at least you reached back in time.

My sincere sympathy and condolences to you and other members of your family, especially your mother.

Yours sincerely,

Indira Gandhi

(Indira Gandhi)

Dr. K.P. Mathur,
c/o Dr. V.P. Mathur,
K.P.M. Hospital,
Kanpur.

Condolences from PM

LAST, TRAGIC SHOTS

Sanjay Gandhi was very busy with the elections in 1980 which brought Indira Gandhi back into power. The Janata government had begun to crack early on in its term. They were a disparate group of individuals who were bound together by the glue of their common hatred for Indira Gandhi and Sanjay Gandhi and they wanted to teach them a lesson. They were also ambitious and they wanted to make their presence felt. This was not enough to keep them together.

When she became PM again, it was not a very lucky start for her. The biggest setback for her was that Sanjay Gandhi died in a plane crash on 2 June 23, 1980. Strangely enough, she was not overmuch devastated by his death. Within four years, alas, she herself was assassinated.

Before she entered PM's house for the fourth time, some of her well-meaning friends had organized a *havan* to exorcise any evil spirits. This function was held for a full couple of days, not for an hour or two. But it seems some of them remained behind, lurking in the corner.

PM was religious, as has been mentioned earlier. She was superstitious as well. For example, when Maneka was expecting and there was a solar eclipse, she did not want her to be exposed to it. Many years ago, when Jawaharlal Nehru wanted to move into Teen Murti Bhawan from 4, York Road, where he had stayed earlier, she had insisted that he could move there only at a certain date and time fixed by a pandit of Allahabad. An agnostic Nehru had to agree.

She did appear pale and broken after Sanjay's death but only for a few days. Later, she regained her composure and her office and party work went on as usual. As Dhawan has said, no file was delayed. She did not lose sleep or appetite. But she was undoubtedly very much affected. The day after Sanjay died, I saw her in the morning as usual and she said: "*Doctor, hamara dahina haath kat gaya hai* (doctor, my right hand is severed)". She was so much dependent on Sanjay's advice.

It took one full year for her to get Rajiv into politics. This was on her mind even earlier. My feeling is that she was not completely satisfied with Sanjay's thinking and activities. Even during the Emergency days, she used to show her disappointment and disgust. Sometimes she would get agitated and show her disapproval by saying: "Who is doing all this?" Of course, she knew who was behind it. Still, she did not quite approve of everything that Sanjay did.

Rajiv was not interested in politics. He was essentially a family man and was most at home with his family and friends. He had a life of his own which had nothing to do with politics or administration.

Rajiv was persuaded to come into politics after Sanjay's death by a number of people, including many family friends. I was also one among them. I had told him that he must join politics as PM was alone. He didn't say no but I could see that he was reluctant.

Whenever this subject was broached in the presence of Sonia, she did react. To some people she would say: "Rajiv and I have made our life together. Why should we get into this?"

The situation in the country was quite bad when PM took charge for the fourth time. There was trouble in Punjab and Assam, to name just two places. Dalits were facing many atrocities and communal issues were far from resolved. Christians were also complaining of ill-treatment.

In Assam there were riots and a student movement was going on. It was solved by Rajiv Gandhi after he became PM. The mistake that the Congress made in Punjab was because Sanjay Gandhi and Giani Zail Singh, who served as the CM of Punjab and later Union Home Minister, did not discourage Bhindranwale to counter the Akalis.

Initially, Bhindranwale was favourable to the Congress and campaigned for them in the elections, but later he wanted to be independent.

The question of a separate Sikh state had also come up in a big way at around that time and the Anantpur Sahib resolution was passed demanding a separate Khalistan.

PM was unhappy with the situation in Jammu and Kashmir also, where Farooq Abdullah had taken over as CM. She did not think much of him and disliked his flamboyant lifestyle and behaviour. She believed he was in league with the separatists.

She was not happy with the functioning of N.T. Rama Rao of Andhra Pradesh, who had started the Telugu Desam Party, either. She felt they wanted to secede and that is why they had named their party as such. In the same way, the Dravidian parties were also making their presence felt in Tamil Nadu. M.G. Ramachandran had already established himself as a leader of the DMK. They were also also quite strident in their pro-Tamil agenda and ideology. Although the South had always been as a bastion of the Congress, during those days it seemed to be slipping out of her hands. PM very much wanted Rajiv to enter politics and assist her.

Rajiv's entry, thus, helped her regain her poise and composure. By the time Sanjay died and these things happened, PM was losing her self-confidence. Her agility of mind had diminished and her grip on the situation had weakened.

Although Rajiv was a decent, well-meaning and kind-hearted person, he was a political novice.

Within a couple of years of Sanjay's death, Maneka had to leave PM's house under rather trying circumstances. After Sanjay's death, PM's attitude towards her softened a great deal. In fact, she wanted Maneka to come and help her in politics.

But Maneka was often in the company of people who were antagonistic to Rajiv. This grew into the formation of the organization, the Sanjay Vichar Manch (SVM). It was an organization which wanted to carry on with the legacy of Sanjay Gandhi. Maneka and her associates were part of it. They were known to be acting against Rajiv although I never came to know what specifically they were doing.

What brought matters to a head was a convention of the Sanjay Vichar Manch which was held in Lucknow. Maneka was asked to address it. PM was not particularly pleased with her participation in that organization and she even advised her against it, by sending a message, as she was at that time touring abroad. However, Maneka went ahead and addressed the convention.

Maneka was also running a magazine at that time, called *Surya*, along with her mother, which she sold off to two leaders with right-wing links. The magazine was launched in 1976 and continued to come out even during the Janata regime. However, following the death of Sanjay Gandhi, it ran into losses. The sale of the magazine had also gone down.

It was a trashy and low-brow magazine which would not do any credit to any journalist to associate with. In one issue, for instance, there was an exposé about a sex scandal involving Jagjivan Ram's son, Suresh Ram, in 1978. Jagjivan Ram had quit the Congress by then to become a senior minister in Janata government. Nandini Satpathy and H.N. Bahuguna were others who had left the Congress party along with him. Even Mrs Vijayalakshmi Pandit joined the new political grouping, called the Congress for Democracy, along with these three. The CFD contested elections together with the Janata Party and later merged in it. They had named their party as if democracy was not on Indira Gandhi's side. The exposé was said to have hurt Jagjivan Ram's political career. The magazine had also run a gossip item on Rani Jethmalani, daughter of the lawyer Ram Jethmalani, which had led to a law suit, with adverse results for the magazine which had to render an abject apology.

The relations between PM and Vijayalakshmi Pandit were always strained, as mentioned earlier. Mrs Pandit had made certain remarks in the past about PM's looks and her intellectual caliber. Normally blood is thicker than water but in this case, blood turned into water at the sight of ambition fulfilled.

Rajiv was already there in a big way. He started to take charge of everything and he became PM's main advisor.

Meanwhile, the Punjab crisis had begun to gather momentum. Bhindranwale's gang was acquiring an upper hand. Sikhs were getting alienated. Hindu-Sikh tension was increasing. Bhindranwale and his people had occupied a small part of the periphery in the Golden Temple.

Many Hindu leaders were shot dead. Some of the Sikh leaders also, considered pro-Congress were killed. There was a rumour that Bhindranwale had a list of people who were to be shot. Small chits bearing their names were put in a bowl. A follower was asked to pick one of them, and go and shoot the person whose name came up. Killings occurred not only in Punjab but other parts of the country as well. At one stage he said that rice will not be sent out of Punjab. There was a lot of fear in Punjab and Hindus started to leave the state and take refuge in Haryana.

Arun Nehru and Arun Singh were amongst others who were advising the Prime Minister on the Punjab crises. There view was that the negotiations will not help. They were in favour of some positive action. Ultimately, action was taken. PM was worried but she was getting no sound advice from any quarter. One morning, having read some horrendous report about the killings in Punjab, I mentioned them to PM when I went to see her. She had apparently also seen that report in the newspapers. We were in her sitting room. She went inside but came back in no time with a newspaper in hand and a nail clipper. She sat down on the carpet, spread the newspaper in front of her, put her foot on it and started to clip her nails. Perhaps she wanted to get it off her chest, while not wanting to let me know what exactly was being done in response to what she had heard from me.

Although PM continued to act normal after the military intervention in Amritsar, which caused great damage and causalities, it did appear that something had been sucked out of her. She did not seem at peace with what had happened. She was asked to change her Sikh bodyguards but she refused saying it could not be done in a secular country. However, the Indo-Tibetan Border Force was added to her personal security.

The day before she was assassinated, we had returned from Bhubaneshwar from a campaign for the next assembly elections. It was a two-day trip.

Despite all strains of the previous day she appeared quite alright, although she was tired from her trip. I mentioned to her how happy the ADC'S wife was who had met her the previous evening at Raj Bhawan. She complained of a cold and I gave her some medicines. I came out from her room and found that in the visitor's room two beauticians from the Doordarshan were waiting for her makeup for her interview with Peter Ustinov.

We all sat down together and some tea was ordered. When the beauticians were busy with her I mentioned having read in the *Time* magazine, which I was reading on the aircraft, that American President Ronald Reagan has refused to put any makeup before his TV interviews. But PM contradicted it. She also said that Reagan used to have an earpiece affixed while being interviewed, over which he was prompted advice before answering questions put by journalists. Out of the blue she remembered of my daughter having topped in high school several years earlier. After the makeup was over PM got up and went inside to get ready to go for the interview. She gave some instructions to her valet, Nathuram for a dress change to receive the President at the airport in the evening. After that, I left for the hospital. As soon as I reached, my PA who had received a telephone message from PM's house called about some shoot-out incident and said PM was also injured. I reversed the car and went to PM's house; by that time she had already been taken to the All India Institute of Medical Sciences. When I reached AIIMS, I found her oozing blood. I think she was already dead.

With her death, my assignment also came to an end. I was to retire in December 1983. A few months before that, I thought it prudent to let her know about my impending retirement. I thought if I tell her on the day itself, two things could happen: either she would say please don't go, I need you; the other thing could be, if you are retired, go, so what? I did not want either of the two things to happen. I did not want a PM to request me to stay on. Nor did I want to be dismissed curtly. So I informed her well in time. At that time, she decided she would give me two more years in service, till the next elections, due in 1985. She told P.C. Alexander, her secretary, that she wanted me to stay till the balance of the term and would decide what to do after that accordingly. But I could avail of only one year of the extension.

PRIME MINISTER
INDIA

New Delhi
January 6, 1985

Dear Dr. Mathur,

During your service with Government you took such good care of us and of so many others. Now that you have retired, may I wish you many more years of active life?

Yours sincerely,

(Rajiv Gandhi)

Dr. K.P. Mathur,
C-1/6, Lodi Gardens,
New Delhi - 110 003.

A letter from Rajiv Gandhi

ABOVE At the mausoleum of President of Romania. Dr Mathur also seen in the picture

BELOW Mrs Gandhi with some officials of the church who had called on her on Christmas Eve

ABOVE With Dr Danton Cooley, the famous cardiologist. Dr Mathur and Dr Khalilullah look on

BELOW During a visit to one of the naval bases. Author also in the pic

ABOVE Meeting a delegation of foreign Indian residents in Europe

BELOW Dr Mathur with Maneka Gandhi and President Zail Singh's daughter

ABOVE During a visit to a museum in Athens

BELOW President and Mrs Reagan bidding goodbye after a banquet, Dr Mathur paying respects to President Reagan. Also seen is Zubin Mehta

FACING PAGE During a visit to a flower show on a foreign visit

ABOVE Laying a wreath in Burma on the photo of an ex-leader

BELOW Accepting a salute at a naval base

Planting a sapling in Bulgaria

ABOVE During a visit to a museum in Cairo. Dr Mathur in the background

BELOW With President and Nancy Reagan at a banquet in the White House

At a military station in Himachal Pradesh. Dr Y.S. Parmar, Chief Minister in the pic. Author also in the background

ABOVE With Dr Mathur and other doctors and a nurse during one of her annual checkups.

BELOW At a children's hospital in Maldives. Dr Mathur in background

ABOVE Dining with naval officers on board *SS Mysore*, Dr Mathur sitting at the head of the table

BELOW Signing Charter of Health in WHO Headquarters, Geneva. Dr Mathur looks on

ABOVE At a function in Bombay. Also seen are Rajni Patel, General Secretary, Congress Party, Mr Naik, Chief Minister of Maharashtra, Dr Banerjee, MD of Sandoz (India) and Dr Mathur

BELOW At her home with a foreign visitor. Dr Mathur looks on

SELECT GLOSSARY OF NAMES

Anandamayi Ma: Born in 1896 in Bengal, Anandamayi Ma was one of the most influential spiritual personalities of the last century. Among her devotees were prime ministers, Nehru and Indira Gandhi.

Arun Nehru: Politician and columnist he also became a business leader. Was elected to the Lok Sabha on a Congress ticket and became a member of Rajiv Gandhi's Cabinet, as HRD minister. He fell out with the party and joined the Janata party.

B.K. Nehru: A former ambassador to the US, he was a cousin of Nehru. He qualified for the ICS and was awarded the Padma Bhushan.

Bansi Lal: Congress strong man and chief minister of Haryana, he is considered the architect of modern Haryana. He became Union Defence Minister as well and was a close friend of Sanjay Gandhi.

Bibi Amtus Salam: A disciple of Mahatma Gandhi and social worker, she played an active role in the rehabilitation of the displaced people during partition. She also played a major role in combating communal violence during those charged times.

Col. R.D. Ayyar: The first medical superintendent of Safdarjung General hospital, and a family physician to the Jawaharlal Nehru family, he became the director-general of the Central Government Health Services.

Dheerendra Brahmachari: Yoga teacher to Indira Gandhi, this yoga exponent hailed from Bihar and ran a number of schools to teach the science.

Fakhruddin Ali Ahmed: The son of an army doctor from Assam, Ahmed was educated in India and studied history at the University of Cambridge. Graduating in 1927 he returned to India he was elected to the Assam assembly in 1935, becoming the state minister of finance and revenue in 1938.

Indira Gandhi included him in her first cabinet in January 1966 and he held a variety of portfolios—irrigation and power, education, industrial development, and agriculture. He became the fifth President in 1974.

Firaq Gorakhpuri: Eminent poet, writer, critic and, according to one commentator, one of the most noted Urdu poets of contemporary India, Firaq established himself among peers including Muhammad Iqbal, Yagana Changezi, Jigar Moradabadi and Josh Malihabadi.

Gayatri Devi: The London-born princess of Cooch Behar was the third Maharani of Jaipur from 1939 to 1970 after her marriage to Maharaja Sawai Man Singh II. Gayatri Devi entered active politics on an anti-Congress plank when she founded the Swatantra Party. She won a landslide victory to the Lok Sabha from Jaipur in 1962 and again in 1971.

General Manekshaw: Sam Hormusji Framji Jamshedji Maneskshaw, popularly known as Sam Bahadur, was the first Indian Army officer to be promoted to the five-star rank of Field Marshal. **Well-known** for his bravery and forthright approach, Manekshaw was promoted to the rank of Field Marshal in 1973. He was also a recipient of the Padma Vibhushan, Padma Bhushan and the Military Cross.

H.N. Bahuguna: He was jailed as part of Quit India movement from 1942 to 1946. He joined the Union Cabinet and was made State Minister for Communication in 1971. In 1973, he became UP Chief Minister but it was a short tenure. And he quit in 1975. When Emergency was lifted and elections called he quit the Congress and formed a new group, the Congress for Democracy with Jagjivan Ram and Nandini Satpathy which joined the Janata Party. In 1980, he won from Garhwal as Congress (I) candidate. but soon left and resigned his seat.

H.Y. Sharada Prasad: Known mostly for his long association with Indira Gandhi, the Bangalore-born writer began life as a journalist. After working with the Express group, he joined Publications Division as Assistant Editor and went on to edit Planning Commission's journal '*Yojana.*' It was during this stint that Indira Gandhi picked him to join her staff.

Jagjivan Ram: Endearingly called babuji, this independence activist and politician from Bihar was instrumental in forming the All-India Depressed Classes League, dedicated to attaining equality for untouchables. He was elected to Bihar Assembly in 1937. He was Defence Minister during the Indo-Pak war of 1971. His contribution to the Green Revolution and modernizing agriculture, during his two tenures as agriculture minister are still remembered, especially during the 1974 drought when he was asked to hold the additional portfolio to tide over the food crisis.

Though he supported Indira Gandhi during the Emergency, he left Congress in 1977 and joined the Janata Alliance. He later became Deputy Prime Minister (1977–79).

Jarnail Singh Bhindranwale: A leader of the Damdami Taksal (a Sikh religious group) and notable for his support of the Anandpur Sahib Resolution, he advocated against the consumption of liquor, drugs and laxness in religious practices. He condemned Article 25 of the Constitution declaring minorities such as Sikhs, Jains and Buddhists as part of Hinduism.

Jayaprakash Narayan: Popularly known as JP or Lok Nayak, for the role he played during the Emergency days, Narayan was an independence activist, social reformer and political leader. He is remembered for his role in the overthrow of the Indira regime through what he called a "total revolution". He was posthumously awarded the Bharat Ratna. Other awards include the Magsaysay award for Public Service. The Patna airport is also named after him as also the largest hospital run by the Delhi government.

K.C. Pant: A former Planning Commission deputy chairman and defence minister, Pant was in the Rajiv Gandhi Cabinet from 1987 to 1989 at a crucial time when the Indian Peace Keeping Forces were deployed in Sri Lanka.

Mohammad Yunus: A Padma Bhushan awardee, he was a member of Indian Foreign Service and served as envoy in Turkey, Indonesia, Spain and Iraq. He also organized trade fairs and headed the Trade Fair Authority of India and was instrumental in the setting up of the exhibition complex at Pragati Maidan in New Delhi.

Morarji Desai: The first Prime minister to head a non-Congress government from 1977 to 1979, he also held many key positions earlier; as chief minister of Bombay and as finance and home minister at the Centre.

Desai made notable efforts to initiate peace between arch rivals Pakistan and India. After India's first nuclear explosion in 1974, he helped restore friendly relations with China and Pakistan, and vowed to avoid armed conflict such as the Bangladesh war. Desai closed down much of the premier intelligence agency Research and Analysis Wing and reduced its budget and operations. He is the only Indian leader to be conferred Pakistan's highest civilian award, *Nishan-e-Pakistan*, in 1990.

N.K. Seshan: Private secretary to the first prime minister, Jawaharlal Nehru.

Nandini Satpathy: While a student at Ravenshaw College in Cuttack she became involved in the Communist Party's student wing, the Student Federation of India. After Indira Gandhi became Prime Minister in 1966, Satpathy became a minister attached to the Prime Minister, with her specific portfolio of Ministry of Information and Broadcasting.

Navin Chawla: A former Chief Election Commissioner of India; four phases (out of five) of the lok sabha elections in 2009 were executed under his supervision in April and May that year. Chawla, however, is best known for his biography of Mother Teresa and for conducting the 2009 elections in an even-handed manner to all round acclaim.

P.C. Alexander: In a remarkable career spanning six decades, P.C. Alexander was Principal Secretary to two Prime Ministers, Indian High Commissioner to Britain, Governor of Tamil Nadu and Maharashtra, a United Nations civil servant and also a Rajya Sabha MP.

When Indira Gandhi returned to power in 1980, she handpicked him to become Principal Secretary and, in the process, her political adviser and administrative trouble-shooter.

Padmaja Naidu: Daughter of the feisty poet Sarojini Naidu, Padmaja joined the Indian National Congress at the young age of 21. She became the founder of the party in Hyderabad and was imprisoned during the Quit India movement in 1942. She was active in propagating the use of khadi and boycott of foreign goods. After Independence, she was elected to Parliament but left on health grounds. She was Governor of West Bengal and was also chairperson of the Indian Red Cross. During the Bangaldesh war she played a crucial role in helping the displaced persons, especially women.

Pupul Jayakar: A friend and biographer of the Nehru-Gandhi family and a close associate of the philosopher, J. Krishnamurti, Jayakar had a close relationship with three prime ministers: Nehru, Indira Gandhi and son Rajiv. She served as cultural adviser to two, and presided over the country's cultural scene for nearly 40 years. She founded institutions promoting talented artists and crafts through festivals and exhibitions worldwide, including the India festivals in major cities in the West. She received the Padma Bhushan in 1967.

R.K. Dhawan: A former private secretary to Indira Gandhi and a witness to the assassination of the prime minister, he became an MP from Bihar. During the Emergency he wielded enormous power.

R.K. Nehru: A member of the Indian Civil Service, he was ambassador in China. He was a cousin of Pandit Nehru.

Raj Narain: A colourful Socialist leader who defeated Indira Gandhi in a Lok Sabha election and played a key role in the fall of a successor, Narain was active in the independence movement. He was later imprisoned scores of times for his leadership of opposition movements. **In 1975,** a high court upheld Mr Narain's charges of electoral fraud against Mrs Gandhi. That verdict led to the clamping down of Emergency. Two years later, when Mrs Gandhi called for new elections, Mr Narain and his colleagues rode a popular wave of unrest to defeat her. In the new Morarji Desai Government, Mr Narain was appointed Health Minister. He set about changing the policy on family planning and renounced forced sterilizations.

Rukhsana Sultana: a social worker, socialite and friend of Sanjay Gandhi she came into prominence during the Emergency in connection with the sterilizations imposed by the regime, especially in the Old Delhi area.

Sheikh Mujibur Rahman: The son of a middle-class landowner, Sheikh Mujib studied law and political science at the Universities of Calcutta and Dacca. He was jailed briefly as a teenager for agitating for Indian independence. He began his formal political career in 1949 as a co-founder of the Awami League that advocated political autonomy for East Pakistan. Mujib demanded independence for East Pakistan. Troops from West Pakistan were sent to regain control of the eastern province but were defeated. East Pakistan, renamed Bangladesh, was proclaimed an independent republic in 1971, and in January 1972, Mujib became the country's first prime minister.

Sheila Kaul: A social democratic leader of the Indian National Congress, a stateswoman, cabinet minister and governor, and the oldest living former member of parliament at the time of her death, Sheila Kaul was also an educator, social worker, and social reformer in Uttar Pradesh. She was Jawaharlal Nehru's sister-in-law and Indira Gandhi's maternal aunt.

Siddhartha Shankar Ray: Eminent barrister and chief minister of West Bengal during the Naxalbari agitation, he used strong-arm methods against Jadavpur University students. He was also Governor of Punjab and became Union Education Minister and was a confidant of Indira Gandhi. He was reported to have drafted the document that ushered in the Emergency.

Subhadra Joshi: Born on March 23, 1919 in Sialkot (now in Pakistan), she was one of the veterans of the freedom struggle. During Partition she set up a peace volunteer organization 'Shanti Dal' which went from door to door spreading Gandhiji's message of peace and amity. She also organized rehabilitation of evacuees from Pakistan.

T.N. Kaul: A former Foreign Secretary, Mr Kaul also served as Ambassador to the US as well as the Soviet Union. An ICS officer of the 1939 batch, he had a distinguished career serving as India's Ambassador to the USSR twice, and also to Iran and as Deputy High Commissioner in London. He was also Vice-Chairman of the UNESCO and Chairman of the Indian Council for Cultural Relations.

Tarkeshwari Sinha: Among the first women political activists from her state, she took active role in the Quit India Movement. At the age of 26, she was elected to the 1st Lok Sabha from Patna East in 1952. She was re-elected in 1957, 1962 and 1967 from Barh and became the first woman deputy finance minister in the Nehru Cabinet (1954–64). She led a delegation to the UN and Tokyo.

Vijayaraje Scindia: An active politician belonging to the Jana Sangh and later Bharatiya Janata Party, she ruled one of the largest and richest princely states for years and was the Rajmata of Gwalior, spouse of the last ruling Maharaja of Gwalior, Jiyajirao Scindia.

During Emergency, Scindia was imprisoned in Tihar Jail where she served as a political prisoner. With this began differences with her son Madhavrao who left India and went to Nepal to stay with his sister. After the Emergency was lifted, he returned back to India and joined Congress. The year 1980 proved beneficial for Scindia when she became one of the Vice Presidents of BJP and she provided full support to the Ayodhya theme and continued in that post till 1998.

Yashpal Kapoor: Private secretary to Prime Minister Indira Gandhi, he was charged with misuse of his position during the election for working for Mrs Gandhi. A Rajya Sabha member, he also became manager of the *National Herald* newspaper published from Delhi.

Zail Singh: The seventh President, serving from 1982 to 1987, Singh was a politician with the Indian National Congress and held several ministerial posts in the Union Cabinet, including that of Home Minister. He was also earlier Chief Minister of Punjab. His presidency was marked by Operation Bluestar, the assassination of Indira Gandhi, and the 1984 anti-Sikh riots. He died of injuries sustained in 1994 after a car accident.

ACKNOWLEDGEMENTS

This book is a labour of love, a culmination of my life's experiences and efforts. I am immensely grateful to Abhimanyu Kumar Singh, a fine and diligent young man and a journalist with a curious mind who helped me in putting the manuscript together. My love and gratitude to my daughters and grandchildren for their encouragement and support throughout this journey. I appreciate the patience of my eldest daughter, Mala Mathur, who sat through many sessions during making the manuscript. I thank Konark Publishers Pvt Ltd, my publishers for putting such faith in the manuscript. Thank you, Mr K.P.R. Nair and Priyanka Sarkar for this lovely book.

And last but not the least, to Indira Gandhiji for all the memories.